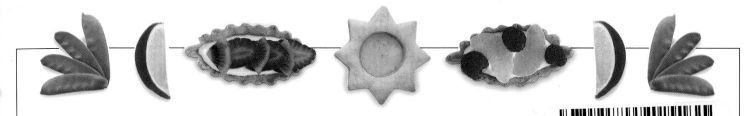

CHILDREN'S QUICK & EASY COOK BOOK

BY
ANGELA WILKES

DK

DK PUBLISHING, INC.

EDITORS
Rachel Harrison, Mary Atkinson

ART EDITORS
Mary Sandberg, Claire Penny

ADDITIONAL DESIGN
Michelle Baxter, Susan Calver,
Karen Chapman, Helen Melville

DEPUTY MANAGING ART EDITOR
Jane Horne

SENIOR MANAGING EDITOR
Sheila Hanly

PHOTOGRAPHY
Amanda Haywood, Clive Streeter,
Norman Hollands, Dave King

HOME ECONOMISTS
Nicola Fowler, Emma Jane Frost,
Emma Patmore

US EDITORS
Laaren Brown, Kristin Ward

PRODUCTION
Josie Alabaster

DTP DESIGNERS
Almudena Díaz, Nicola Studdart

This American Edition, 2019
First American Edition, 1997
Published in the United States by DK Publishing
1450 Broadway, Suite 801,
New York, NY 10018

Copyright © 1997, 2019, Dorling Kindersley Limited,
DK, a Division of Penguin Random House LLC
17, 16
060–KR150–Aug/2006
Text copyright © 1997 Angela Wilkes

A catalog record for this book
is available from the Library of Congress.
ISBN: 978-0-7566-1814-8

Color reproduction by Bright Arts, Hong Kong
Printed and bound in China

DK would like to thank:
Emma Price-Thomas, Rachel Wardley, and
Sarah Phillips for additional editorial help;
Amanda Harrold, Nicola Harrold, Stacey Martin,
Sarah Mendham, Natasha Payne, Sam Priddy,
and David Watts for modeling.

A WORLD OF IDEAS:
SEE ALL THERE IS TO KNOW

www.dk.com

CONTENTS

SUPER-FAST SNACKS

BAGEL BONANZA   12
These traditional chewy rolls can
have sweet or savory fillings and
make an ideal breakfast or snack.

CROISSANT FEAST   13
Delicious, buttery French croissants
filled with rich cream and jam,
chocolate, or ham and cheese.

CRUNCHY CROSTINI   14
Little pieces of Italian-style toasted
bread with lots of tasty toppings
to choose from.

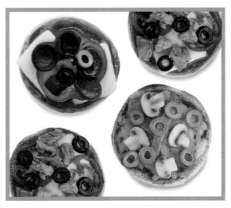

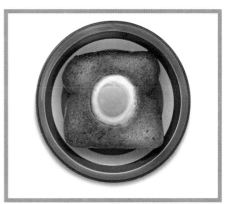

SPEEDY MEALS

CLASSIC OMELETS 26-27
Two very different omelets: a quick cheese omelet and a tasty Spanish omelet, called a tortilla.

PERFECT PASTA 32-33
Pasta and sliced sausages baked in a delicious tomato sauce make this a hearty evening meal.

FISHCAKE FLOUNDERS 36-37
Tasty tuna and potato fishcakes are cooked with a crunchy crust made from fresh bread crumbs.

VEGETABLE SOUPS 28-29
Two tasty vegetable soups: a summery minted pea soup and a thick carrot and orange soup.

TURKISH MEATBALLS 34
Spicy Middle Eastern meatballs made from ground lamb and grilled on skewers.

CHICKEN NUGGETS 38
Bite-sized nuggets of tender chicken coated in fresh bread crumbs and fried.

TACOS AND GUACAMOLE 30-31
Crisp Mexican pancakes with two spicy fillings and an avocado dip.

FALAFEL 35
Spicy chickpea fritters packed into pita bread and served with minted yogurt, cucumber, and tomato.

LEMONY FISH STICKS 39
A crisp lemon-and-herb coating makes these fresh fish sticks a tasty change to store-bought varieties.

BARBECUED BITES   40-41
Marinated spare ribs, tomato kebabs, and seasoned corn to cook on a barbecue or under a grill.

THAI KEBABS WITH SATAY SAUCE   46-47
Thai-style pork, chicken, and shrimp kebabs with a peanut butter sauce.

CARROT SALAD   51
A really crunchy salad made with grated carrots, lots of raisins, and toasted sunflower seeds.

CHICKEN CHOW MEIN   42-43
Chinese noodles stir-fried with sliced chicken and lots of vegetables.

SALADE NIÇOISE   48-49
This salad from the south of France, made with tuna, potatoes, tomatoes, and olives, is a light meal in itself.

FILLED CREPES   52-53
A basic light crepe recipe and two ideas for savory fillings: ham and cheese or creamy mushroom.

CHICKEN CURRY AND RICE   44-45
A mild and creamy chicken curry served with spicy rice.

TABBOULEH   50
This exotic salad from north Africa is made with bulgur wheat, cucumber, mint, and parsley.

SPICY CHICKEN BURGERS   54
Fried spicy chicken served in a sesame-seed bun with lettuce, sour cream, and tomato relish.

DELIGHTFUL DESSERTS

CREAM PUFFS   56-57
A pile of light, easy-to-make buns filled with whipped cream and smothered in chocolate sauce.

LEMON CHEESECAKE   60-61
A wonderfully light, lemon-flavored cheesecake baked in the oven, then chilled in the refrigerator.

FRUIT CRUMBLE   64
This traditional baked dessert has a juicy apple-and-blackberry filling and a crunchy topping.

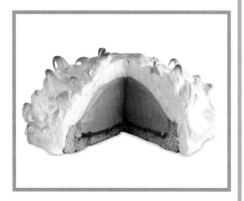

BAKED ALASKA   58
A magical mound of ice cream, sponge cake, and snowy peaks of meringue, baked in the oven.

TIRAMISU   62
A rich Italian dessert made with rich soft cheese, sponge cake, coffee, and grated chocolate.

FRUIT SALAD   65
Fresh pineapple, melon, grapes, and mango give this fruit salad an exciting tropical flavor.

KNICKERBOCKER GLORIES   59
Tall, cool ice-cream sundaes: strawberry or banana flavor.

CLAFOUTI   63
This traditional French dessert is made with fresh plums baked in a bed of sponge cake.

HOT CHOCOLATE SOUFFLÉS   66
An easy recipe for making four impressive little chocolate soufflés.

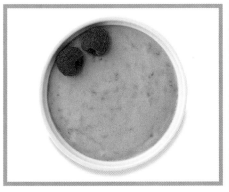

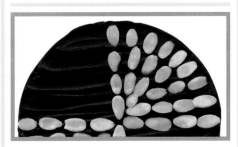

TREATS AND SWEETS

RASPBERRY FOOLS　　67
A delicious and very quick summer dessert made of crushed raspberries and whipped cream.

ULTIMATE CHOCOLATE CAKE　72-73
A rich, gooey chocolate-and-almond cake that would impress a top chef.

OAT BARS　　78-79
Three varieties of this popular crunchy bar cookie: plain, fruit-and-nut, and chocolate-dipped.

TOTALLY TERRIFIC TRIFLE　　68-69
An old-favorite dessert made with sponge cake, fruit, custard, and cream.

FROSTED CARROT CAKE　　74-75
A delicious, moist cake with cream-cheese frosting and fun decorations.

STAINED-GLASS COOKIES 80
These amazing shortbread cookies with "stained-glass" centers look festive and taste good, too.

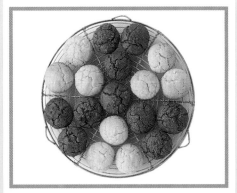

FRUITY CRÈME BRÛLÉES　　70
Fresh fruit topped with creamy yogurt and a crisp caramel crust.

MACAROONS　　76-77
These little almond cookies melt in your mouth. Choose between plain macaroons or the chocolate variety.

CHOCOLATE DIPS　　81
Fresh orange zest gives these simple yet elegant cookies a subtle zing that goes well with the chocolate tip.

RASPBERRY MUFFINS   82
Delicious, puffy snacking muffins studded with raspberries and nuggets of white chocolate.

FLORENTINES   86
Exotic cookies made from chopped fruit and nuts set in toffee and coated with chocolate.

FRUIT-AND-NUT BALLS 89
Apricots, raisins, almonds, coconut, and white chocolate flavor these tasty little sweets.

PECAN PUFFS   83
Irresistible, light-as-a-feather cookies made from pecan nuts and dusted with confectioners' sugar.

CHOCOLATE CRISPY CAKES   87
Really easy cakes to make, using just breakfast cereal and chocolate.

PEANUT BUTTER TREATS   90
Fudgy, peanut butter-flavored treats coated in chocolate.

TEMPTING TARTS   84-85
Two types of tart: simple jam tarts and more sophisticated fresh fruit and cream tarts.

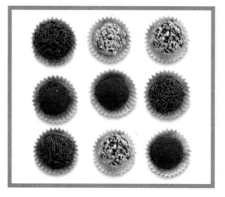

CHOCOLATE TRUFFLES 88
A quick and easy version of these famous chocolate candies with three delicious coatings.

PEPPERMINT CREAMS 91
Easy-to-make, peppermint-flavored candies in pretty pastel colors or dipped in chocolate.

BEFORE YOU START

The CHILDREN'S QUICK AND EASY COOKBOOK is packed full of delicious, easy-to-follow recipes that anyone can make. From tasty snacks to scrumptious desserts, there is something for every occasion.

HOW TO USE THIS BOOK

You will find a quick description of all the recipes in the book on pages 2 to 8. Every recipe lists the equipment and ingredients you need, and shows you step-by-step exactly what to do. All the main cooking terms are shown in italic type, like this: *simmer*. You can look up the meaning of these cooking terms in the step-by-step picture glossary on pages 92 to 95.

WEIGHING AND MEASURING

Every recipe gives both imperial and metric measurements. Use only one set of measurements throughout a recipe, as it is not possible to convert one set of measurements to the other exactly. A "spoonful" in this book means a level spoonful.

USING THE OVEN

Always ask an adult to turn on the oven for you. Sometimes the oven needs to be switched on to the temperature given in the recipe before you start cooking, so it has time to heat up. This is called preheating. The temperatures for electric ovens are shown in Fahrenheit (°F) and Celsius (°C). Always follow the cooking time given in the recipe, and don't forget to turn off the oven when you are done.

BE CAREFUL!

Never cook anything unless there is an adult to help you. This oven mitt symbol is a safety warning. Whenever you see it next to a picture, ask an adult for help, and remember to be extra careful.

KEY TO SYMBOLS

At the top of each recipe you will see some of the following symbols. They give you quick information about the recipe.

This symbol shows you how long it will take to prepare the recipe.

This symbol shows you how long it will take to cook the food.

This symbol shows you how many people the recipe serves, or what quantity it makes.

This symbol shows you the oven temperature you should use.

KITCHEN RULES

1 Before you start cooking, wash your hands and put on an apron. It's a good idea to roll up your sleeves as well.

2 Gather all the ingredients together. Measure out the dry ingredients and the liquids using measuring cups.

3 Be very careful with sharp knives. Hold them with the blade pointing downward, and always use a cutting board.

4 When you are cooking on top of the stove, turn the pot and pan handles to the side so that you do not bump them.

5 When you are stirring food in a saucepan, use a wooden spoon and hold the saucepan firmly by the handle.

6 Always wear oven mitts when picking up anything hot, or when putting things into or taking them out of the oven.

7 Have a space ready for hot pans. Put them on a trivet or a wooden board, not right onto a table or work surface.

8 Always make sure your hands are dry before you plug in or disconnect an electric appliance, such as a blender.

9 Clean up as you go along, and wipe up any spills right away. Each time you handle a different food, wash your hands afterward.

Super-Fast Snacks

BAGEL BONANZA

You will need

Cutting board • Bread knife
Broiler pan • Knife • Spoon

Ingredients

 1 or 2 bagels
per person

Suggested fillings

Cream cheese

 Sliced salami

Cherry compote

Sliced banana

Grated Cheddar cheese

Sliced tomato

The bottom half of this bagel was
covered in grated cheese, topped
with tomato, and then grilled.

What to do

1 Cut the bagels in half.
Heat the broiler and toast
the bagels lightly, cut sides up,
until the edges are golden brown.

2 Layer the bottoms with the
filling of your choice, then
put the lids on the bagels and
eat them while they're still warm.

To make this
bagel, fill it
with cream
cheese and
sliced salami.

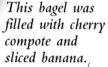

This bagel was
filled with cherry
compote and
sliced banana.

CROISSANT FEAST

You will need

Broiler pan • Cutting board
Bread knife • Butter knife • Grater

Ingredients

 1 or 2 croissants per person

Suggested fillings

Crème fraîche or sour cream

 Strawberry jam

Dark semisweet chocolate

Sliced ham

 Grated Cheddar cheese

Tasty tips

Try different kinds of jam in the jam croissant, or use stewed apple or fruit compote instead. In the cheese croissant, try other cheeses, such as Gruyère.

What to do

Warm the croissants in the oven or under the broiler, then cut them in half and spread with the filling of your choice.

This croissant was made by spreading the base with a layer of crème fraîche and topping it with strawberry jam.

To make this delicious croissant, sprinkle grated dark chocolate on the bottom, warm it under the broiler for a minute, and then add the lid.

Make this delicious croissant by laying a slice of ham on the bottom, sprinkling grated cheese on top, and grilling it for a minute before adding the lid.

13

CRUNCHY CROSTINI

You will need

Cutting board • Bread knife
Broiler pan • Sharp knife
Small bowl • Pastry brush

Ingredients

1 baguette/
French bread stick

1 clove garlic

Olive oil

Suggested toppings

Pizza sauce

Sliced mozzarella cheese

Sliced tomatoes

Hummus

Sliced pitted black olives

Parsley

Pesto

Sliced cherry tomatoes

Canned tuna fish

Chopped celery

Chives

Sliced mozzarella cheese

Sliced ham

Soft cream or
farmer cheese

Sliced salami

What to do

1 Heat the broiler. Carefully cut the baguette into slices, then toast the pieces of bread on both sides until golden brown.

2 Rub one side of each piece of toast with half a clove of garlic, brush it with olive oil, and add the topping of your choice.

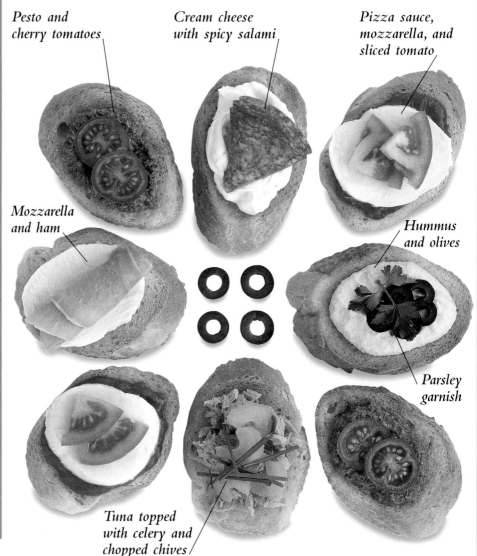

Pesto and
cherry tomatoes

Cream cheese
with spicy salami

Pizza sauce,
mozzarella, and
sliced tomato

Mozzarella
and ham

Hummus
and olives

Parsley
garnish

Tuna topped
with celery and
chopped chives

TRIPLE-DECKER DAGWOODS

You will need

Cutting board • Butter knife
Spoon • Bread knife

Spicy dagwood

3 slices bread

Butter

Sliced cold chicken

Diced cucumber and chopped mint in plain yogurt

Mango chutney

Festive dagwood

3 slices bread

Sliced cold cooked sausage

Mayonnaise

Sliced cold turkey

Cranberry sauce
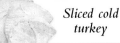

Tricolor dagwood

3 slices bread

Sliced mozzarella cheese
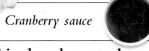

Sliced tomato

Sliced avocado

French dressing

What to do

1 Spread the slices of bread with butter or mayonnaise if you like. Layer half the ingredients over one slice.

2 Add the second slice of bread, then another layer of ingredients. Add the third slice, then cut the sandwich in quarters.

Brown bread was used to make this spicy dagwood.

To make this festive dagwood, spread the bread with mayonnaise. Lettuce can be added for extra color.

A toothpick helps hold the sandwich together.

The tricolor dagwood gets its name from its three bright colors: red, white, and green.

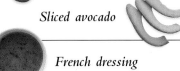

15

POPCORN TREATS

You will need

Large saucepan with lid
Small saucepan • Wooden spoon

Ingredients

 2 tablespoons vegetable oil

 ½ cup (55 g) popcorn

For maple peanut pops

 2 tablespoons butter

 3 tablespoons crunchy peanut butter

 1 tablespoon maple syrup

For cheesy pops

2 tablespoons butter

 ¼ cup (30 g) grated Parmesan cheese

½ teaspoon salt

Popping the corn

1 Heat the vegetable oil in a large saucepan until hot. Add the popcorn, spreading it out to cover the base of the pan.

2 Cook the corn until it starts to pop, then put on the lid. Cook it for 3 more minutes, while shaking the pan.

Maple peanut pops

Melt the butter, peanut butter, and syrup in a small saucepan over low heat. Stir it well, then pour it over the popcorn.

Cheesy pops

Melt the butter in a small pan over low heat. Stir in the grated cheese and salt. Spoon over the popcorn and mix well.

Maple peanut pops

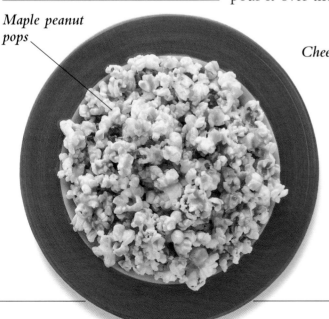

Cheesy pops

FUNKY FRIES

You will need

Small kitchen brush
Cutting board • Sharp knife
Small bowl • Pastry brush
Baking sheet

Ingredients

6 medium
potatoes

4-5 tablespoons
sunflower or olive oil

Salt and pepper

Tasty tips

• To give a Mediterranean flavor to the fries, sprinkle them with dried mixed herbs before cooking them.
• Make delicious parsnip fries by cooking parsnips in the same way as the potatoes.

What to do

1 Preheat the oven. Scrub the potatoes until clean. Cut them in half lengthwise, then cut them into narrow wedges.

2 Brush the baking sheet with oil. Lay the potato wedges in one layer on top, then brush them with oil and *season*.

Mayonnaise
for dipping

3 *Bake* the potato wedges on the top rack of the oven for about 20 minutes or until crisp, golden brown, and puffy.

Funky fries go well with many dishes and make a tasty snack on their own.

Ketchup

PITA POCKETS

You will need

Cutting board • Sharp knife
Broiler pan • Spoon

Ingredients

1 or 2 pita breads
per person

Suggested fillings

Hummus

 Sliced cucumber

Sliced pitted black olives

 Sliced red pepper

Lettuce leaves or
shredded lettuce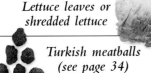

Turkish meatballs
(see page 34)

Yogurt and
mint leaves

Sliced cold chicken

Guacamole (see page 30)

What to do

1 Assemble the ingredients for the filling of your choice. *Chop* or *slice* any ingredients that are not ready to use.

2 Heat the pita breads under the broiler for 1 minute on each side, then slit them open and pack with the filling.

To make this pocket, fill it with guacamole and chicken. Tomato can be added for extra flavor.

The filling in this pocket is shredded lettuce, sliced meatballs, and a dollop of yogurt mixed with chopped mint.

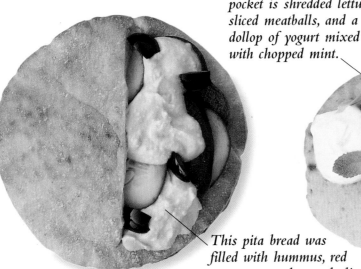

This pita bread was filled with hummus, red pepper, cucumber, and olives.

CHEATER'S PIZZAS

You will need

Broiler pan • Cutting board
Bread knife • Spoon

Ingredients

 1 English muffin per person

 Pizza sauce

Suggested toppings

 Mozzarella cheese

Grated Cheddar cheese

Freshly grated Parmesan cheese

Sliced pepperoni

Strips of ham

Drained canned tuna

Sliced mushrooms

Sliced pitted olives

 Finely sliced red pepper

Sliced tomato

What to do

1 Heat the broiler and toast the English muffins for 1 to 2 minutes on each side. Slice them in half with a bread knife.

2 Put a spoonful of pizza sauce on each English muffin, then spread it evenly across the top.

3 Layer on the toppings you like best, then *grill* the pizzas for a few more minutes until the cheese is melted and bubbly.

To make a tuna pizza, top the muffin with sliced mozzarella, tuna fish, tomato, and black olives.

Make a pepperoni pizza using sliced mozzarella, red pepper, pepperoni, and olives.

This ham-and-cheese pizza was made by sprinkling grated Cheddar cheese on the top, then adding ham, mushrooms, and olives.

19

HOT DOGS WITH SALSA

You will need

Large saucepan • Colander • Cutting board • Bread knife • Sharp knife Spoon • Bowl • Lemon squeezer

For the hot dogs

4 hot dogs

4 hot-dog rolls

For the salsa

½ small onion

3 medium tomatoes

½ lime

A few drops Tabasco sauce

Salt and pepper

Making the hot dogs

1 Heat a large saucepan of water until it *simmers*, then add the hot dogs. Cook them for 5 minutes, then drain.

2 Warm the rolls in the oven for a few minutes, then split each one down the middle. Put a cooked hot dog in each roll.

Making the salsa

1 *Chop* the onion finely. Cut the tomatoes in half, then scoop out and discard the seeds. Chop the tomato flesh finely.

2 Put the chopped tomato in a bowl. Add the onion, the juice of half a lime, the Tabasco, and the *seasoning* and mix well.

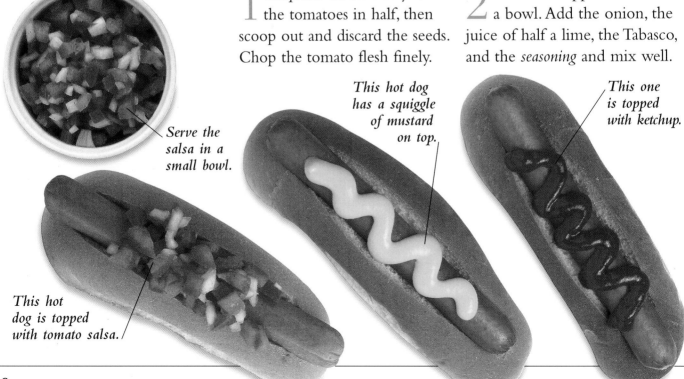

Serve the salsa in a small bowl.

This hot dog has a squiggle of mustard on top.

This one is topped with ketchup.

This hot dog is topped with tomato salsa.

COOL CATS

You will need

Cutting board • Bread knife
Shallow plate • Spoon • Frying pan
Spatula • Broiler pan • Knife

Ingredients

 4 thick slices of French bread

 ½ cup (55 g) all-purpose flour

Salt and pepper

 4 flat, skinned and boned fillets of fish

1 tablespoon vegetable oil

2 tablespoons butter

Butter for spreading

½ lemon

What to do

1 Turn on the broiler. Cut each slice of bread in half. Put the flour on a shallow plate and *season* with salt and pepper.

2 One at a time, lay each fillet of fish in the seasoned flour, turning it over so that it is coated with flour on both sides.

3 Heat the oil and butter in a frying pan. When they are hot, *fry* the fish for about 3 minutes on each side.

4 Warm the bread under the broiler. Butter it. Sandwich each piece of fish in two slices of bread. Add a dash of lemon juice.

Ketchup

Mayonnaise

Serve the Cool Cats with wedges of lemon.

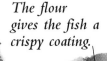

The flour gives the fish a crispy coating.

FRUIT SMOOTHIES

You will need

Cutting board • Sharp knife
Blender or food processor • 2 glasses

Ingredients

1 pint (175 g) strawberries

1 banana

1 lemon

1 tablespoon superfine sugar

½ cup (115 g)
plain yogurt

⅔ cup (150 ml) milk

What to do

Serve the smoothies with colorful drinking straws.

These smoothies are strawberry flavored. For other flavors, try using raspberries or pitted apricots or cherries.

1 Hull, wash, and dry the strawberries. Peel and slice the banana and put it in the blender with a squeeze of lemon.

2 Add the strawberries, sugar, yogurt, and milk. Put the lid on the blender and blend for 1 minute until smooth and frothy.

22

ICE-CREAM SODA

You will need

Glass • Ice-cream scoop or large spoon

Ingredients

 2 scoops strawberry or vanilla ice cream

 ¼ cup (75 ml) strawberry or lime syrup

1 bottle soda water, ginger ale, or other soda

What to do

1 Put 2 scoops of strawberry or vanilla ice cream into a tall glass, then pour strawberry or lime syrup over the top.

2 Slowly pour enough soda water, ginger ale, or other soda on top of the ice cream and syrup to fill the glass.

Strawberry soda made with strawberry ice cream, strawberry syrup, and soda water.

Lime soda made with vanilla ice cream, lime syrup, and lemon-lime soda.

SUNSHINE TOAST

You will need

Cutting board • Cookie cutter
Small bowl • Frying pan • Spatula

Ingredients

1 slice bread

1 egg

2 tablespoons butter

1 tablespoon vegetable oil

What to do

1 Lay the slice of bread down flat and cut a hole in the middle of it with a cookie cutter. Break the egg into a small bowl.

2 Heat the butter and oil in a frying pan. When they are hot, put the bread in the frying pan and *fry* it on one side.

3 Turn the slice of bread over with a spatula, then pour the egg out of the bowl into the hole in the middle of the bread.

4 *Fry* the bread and egg until the egg white is set but the yolk is still runny, then lift it out of the pan onto a plate.

Sunshine toast makes a delicious breakfast on its own or with bacon and tomatoes.

SPEEDY
MEALS

SPEEDY CHEESY OMELET

You will need

Bowl • Whisk or fork • Nonstick frying pan • Spatula • Plate

Ingredients

2 eggs

Salt and pepper

A pat of butter

1 tablespoon grated cheese

Chopped fresh parsley for garnish (optional)

Tasty tips

You can vary the basic omelet recipe by using different fillings.

• To make a ham omelet, use 1 tablespoon of cooked diced ham or bacon instead of cheese.

• To make an herb omelet, use 1 tablespoon chopped fresh parsley and chives instead of cheese.

What to do

1 Break the eggs into a bowl. Add a little salt and pepper, and *beat* the eggs lightly with a whisk or fork until frothy.

2 Melt the butter in a frying pan. When it begins to foam, pour in the eggs, then sprinkle the cheese on top.

3 As the edges of the omelet set, lift them gently and tilt the pan so that the runny egg flows underneath and cooks.

4 When the top has set but is still creamy, loosen the edges of the omelet and fold it in half. Slip it onto a warm plate.

Speedy Cheesy Omelet

Omelet made with chopped ham

Herb omelet flavored with parsley and chives

SPANISH OMELET

You will need

Cutting board • Sharp knife
Nonstick frying pan
Wooden spoon • Mixing bowl
Whisk or fork • Spatula

Ingredients

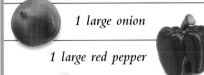

1 large onion

1 large red pepper

2 medium cooked potatoes

2 tablespoons sunflower oil

4 eggs

Salt and pepper

2 tablespoons butter

Tasty tips

For a change, try adding other ingredients to the omelet, such as ¾ cup (115 g) cooked spicy sausage cut into chunks, or ¾ cup (115 g) diced smoked ham.

What to do

1 Peel the onion and *chop* it finely. *Slice* the potatoes. Cut the pepper in half, remove the seeds, and *dice* it.

2 Heat the oil in a frying pan. Cook the onion and pepper gently until soft. Add the potato and cook for 2 minutes.

3 *Beat* the eggs in a bowl. Stir in the onions, peppers, and potatoes, and *season*. Melt the butter in the frying pan.

4 Pour the mixture into the pan. Cook over low heat for about 10 minutes, then cook the top under the broiler.

This omelet is delicious served cold at a picnic.

MINTY PEA SOUP

You will need

Cutting board • Sharp knife
Large saucepan • Wooden spoon
Spoon • Blender or food processor

Ingredients

4 scallions

 4 tablespoons butter

1⅔ cups (450 ml) water

1 lb (450 g)
frozen peas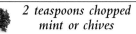

1¼ cups (300 ml)
light cream or milk

2 teaspoons chopped
mint or chives

Salt and pepper

What to do

1 Trim the scallions and *slice* them finely. Melt the butter in a saucepan. Cook the onions over low heat until soft.

2 Add the water. Bring it to a *boil*, then add the peas. *Simmer* for 3 to 4 minutes until the peas are tender.

3 Let the soup cool for a few minutes, then pour it into a blender. Put on the lid and blend until the soup is smooth.

4 Return the soup to the saucepan and stir in the cream and chopped mint or chives. *Season* and reheat gently.

You can serve the soup with a swirl of cream in the middle.

CARROT AND ORANGE SOUP

You will need

Cutting board • Potato peeler
Sharp knife • Grater or zester • Lemon
squeezer • Large saucepan with lid
Blender or food processor • Wooden spoon

Ingredients

1½ lb (675 g) carrots

2 cloves garlic

1 orange

1 lemon

1¼ cups (300 ml) water

Large pinch ground nutmeg

1¼ cups (300 ml) orange juice

1¼ cups (300 ml) light cream

Salt and pepper

What to do

1 Peel and *slice* the carrots. Peel the garlic. Grate the colored part from the orange (this is the zest), and squeeze the lemon.

2 Put the carrots, garlic, zest, orange juice, and water in a pan. Cover and *simmer* for 20 minutes until the carrots are soft.

Garnish the soup with a sprig of parsley or a little grated orange zest.

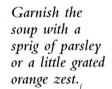

3 Let the soup cool for a few minutes. Add the nutmeg and lemon juice. Pour it into a blender and blend until smooth.

4 Return the soup to the pan, stir in the cream, and add the *seasoning*. Then reheat the soup without letting it *boil*.

TACOS AND GUACAMOLE

You will need

Cutting board • Sharp knife
Garlic press • Large saucepan
Wooden spoon • Baking pan
Spoon • Mixing bowl
Fork • Lemon squeezer

Ingredients

8 taco shells
for each filling

For a meat filling

1 onion

1 clove garlic

2 tablespoons vegetable oil

 1 lb (450 g)
ground beef

1 teaspoon ground cinnamon

½ teaspoon mild chili powder

Salt, pepper, and pinch of oregano

For a bean filling

1 onion

1 carrot

1 clove garlic

2 tablespoons vegetable oil

Salt and pepper

Pinch of cayenne pepper

½ teaspoon mild chili powder

½ teaspoon chili sauce

Squeeze of lemon

14 oz (400 g) canned
chopped tomatoes

 1 lb (450 g) canned
red kidney beans

For the guacamole

2 large, ripe avocados

 1 lime

A few drops chili sauce

Salt and pepper

Making a meat filling

1 Preheat the oven. *Chop* the onion and crush the garlic. Heat the oil in a pan, then cook the onion and garlic until soft.

2 Add the meat. Stir it and cook until brown. Add the oregano, salt, pepper, and spices and cook over low heat for 10 minutes.

Making a bean filling

1 *Chop* the onion, *dice* the carrot, and crush the garlic. Heat the oil, then cook the vegetables until soft, *season,* and stir in dry spices.

2 Stir in the tomatoes, beans, chili sauce, and lemon juice. Cook gently for 15 minutes, or until the sauce has thickened.

Filling the tacos

1 Stand the tacos, open side down, on a baking tray. Put them in the oven for about 3 minutes to warm up.

2 Spoon one of the fillings into the warm taco shells, then garnish with toppings, such as shredded lettuce and grated cheese.

Making the guacamole

1 Cut each avocado in half around its pit, then scoop out the pit with a spoon and peel away the skin.

2 Cut up the avocado flesh and put it into a bowl. Then mash it with a fork to make a smooth, thick paste.

3 Squeeze the lime. Add the lime juice, chili sauce, salt, and pepper to the avocado. Mix everything together until smooth.

Taco toppings

Serve the tacos with small bowls of guacamole, sour cream, and salsa for people to add as extra toppings.

Guacamole

Bean-filled taco garnished with shredded lettuce and grated cheese

Sour cream

Meat-filled taco with scallions, cheese, and lettuce

Prepared salsa

PERFECT PASTA

You will need

Cutting board • Sharp knife • Garlic press • Frying pan • Wooden spoon Large saucepan • Colander • Fork Grill pan • Grater • Baking dish

Ingredients

 1 onion

1 clove garlic

2 tablespoons olive oil

14 oz (400 g) canned tomatoes

1 tablespoon tomato paste

Salt and pepper

Pinch of sugar

 12 oz (340 g) rigatoni or penne

 1 lb (450 g) Italian sausages

 2 slices stale bread

 30 g (1 oz) Cheddar cheese

Tasty tips

• You can vary this recipe by using different pasta shapes. Follow the package directions for cooking.

• If you are cooking for vegetarians, leave out the sausages and increase the amount of cheese used in the topping to 3 oz (85 g).

What to do

1 Preheat the oven. Peel the onion and *chop* it finely. Peel the garlic and crush it or chop it finely. Heat the oil in a frying pan.

2 Cook the onion and garlic over a low heat until soft, then add the canned tomatoes and tomato paste and stir well.

3 Let the pasta sauce *simmer* over low heat for about 10 minutes. Then *season* it with salt, pepper, and a pinch of sugar.

4 *Boil* some salted water in a saucepan. Add the pasta, cook it for about 12 minutes until just soft, and drain it in a colander.

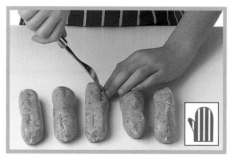

5 Meanwhile, turn on the broiler. Prick the sausages with a fork. *Grill* them on all sides for about 10-12 minutes until brown.

6 Remove the sausages from the broiler, let them stand until cool enough to handle, and cut them into chunky slices.

7 Grate the cheese for the topping. Grate the bread into bread crumbs or else make the bread crumbs in a food processor.

8 Stir the cooked pasta and the sliced sausages into the tomato sauce, then spoon the mixture into a baking dish.

9 Sprinkle the bread crumbs and grated cheese over the pasta. *Bake* for 20 to 25 minutes until the topping is crisp.

Perfect meal

Baked pasta is delicious and very filling, so a simple green salad is all you need to serve with it.

When the pasta is baked, the cheese melts into the bread crumbs, forming a crisp, golden topping.

Rigatoni and penne are tube-shaped, but you can use any other pasta shape you choose.

TURKISH MEATBALLS

You will need

Cutting board • Sharp knife
Garlic press • Mixing bowl • Wooden
spoon • Bamboo skewers • Small bowl
Pastry brush • Broiler pan

Ingredients

1 small onion

1 clove garlic

1 lb (450 g)
ground lamb

A few fresh mint leaves

1 teaspoon ground allspice

1 teaspoon ground cinnamon

Salt and pepper

Vegetable oil for grilling

Handy hints

To prevent the bamboo
skewers from burning, soak
them in water for about
30 minutes before putting
them under a grill or on
a barbecue.

What to do

1 Peel the onion and *chop* it finely. Peel and crush the garlic. Put the onion, garlic, and ground lamb in a mixing bowl.

2 *Chop* the mint finely. Sprinkle the mint, allspice, cinnamon, salt, and pepper over the lamb and mix it into a paste.

3 Split the mixture into 8 portions and mold them into sausage shapes around the skewers. Brush them with oil.

4 Heat the broiler and cook the meatballs for 10 to 12 minutes, turning occasionally until they are brown all over.

Serve the meatballs
on a bed of
shredded lettuce.

Use parsley
leaves as a
garnish.

Lemon wedges
can be squeezed
over the meatballs.

FALAFEL

You will need

Cutting board • Sharp knife • Dish towel
Garlic press • Colander • Large bowl
Fork or food processor • Wooden spoon
Frying pan • Spatula • Paper towels

Ingredients

 1 medium onion

small bunch
flat-leaf parsley

 2 cloves garlic

28 oz (800 g)
canned chickpeas

2 tablespoons
all-purpose flour

1 teaspoon ground coriander

1 teaspoon ground cumin

Vegetable oil
for frying

What to do

1 *Chop* the onion finely. Wash, dry, and *chop* the parsley. Peel and crush the garlic and rinse and drain the chickpeas.

2 Mash the chickpeas with a fork or in a food processor. Mix in the onion, garlic, flour, parsley, coriander, and cumin.

3 With floured hands, roll the mixture into balls about the size of golf balls, then flatten them to make small patties.

4 Heat the oil and *fry* the falafel for a few minutes on each side until golden brown. Drain them on paper towels.

Add chopped mint and a dash of cayenne pepper to plain yogurt and serve it with the falafel.

Serve the falafel in warm pita bread with sliced cucumber and tomato.

FISHCAKE FLOUNDERS

You will need

Cutting board • Vegetable peeler
Sharp knife • Saucepan • Dish towel
Whisk or fork • Small bowl • 3 shallow
bowls or plates • Bowl • Potato masher
Wooden spoon • Frying pan • Spatula

Ingredients

3 medium potatoes

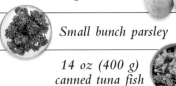 Small bunch parsley

14 oz (400 g) canned tuna fish

2 eggs

½ cup (55 g) all-purpose flour

2 cups fresh bread crumbs

Pat of butter

Salt and pepper

Vegetable oil for frying

Tasty tips

Instead of using tuna, you could
make the fishcakes with canned
salmon. This will give them a
slightly different flavor.

What to do

1 Peel the potatoes, cut them into large chunks, and place in a saucepan of salted water. *Boil* for 12 to 18 minutes until tender.

2 Meanwhile, wash and dry the parsley, cut off the stalks, and *chop* the rest finely. Drain off any liquid from the tuna fish.

3 *Beat* the eggs with a whisk or fork in a small bowl. Put the eggs, flour, and bread crumbs into 3 separate shallow bowls or plates.

4 When the potatoes have cooked, drain off the water and mash them. Stir in the butter and *season* with salt and pepper.

5 Add the tuna fish and the chopped parsley to the mashed potatoes, then stir the mixture together well.

6 Split the tuna mixture into 4 or 8 portions. Roll each one into a ball with your hands, then flatten it into a round fishcake.

7 Turn each fishcake in the flour to coat it completely, then dip it in the beaten egg and finally in the bread crumbs.

8 Heat the vegetable oil in a frying pan. When it is hot, *fry* the fishcakes on both sides until crisp and golden brown.

Fun fish dish

Using green beans and slices of lemon, you can magically turn fishcakes into funny flounders.

Serve the fishcakes with ketchup.

Green beans steamed until tender look like deep-sea plants.

Make an eye out of a slice of green bean.

Use slices of lemon as fish tails.

CHICKEN NUGGETS

You will need

Grater or food processor • 2 shallow bowls or plates • Bowl • Whisk or fork • Cutting board • Sharp knife • Frying pan • Spatula

Ingredients

2 slices stale bread

Salt and pepper

2 eggs

4 skinless chicken breasts

2 tablespoons vegetable oil

Mayonnaise for dipping

Ketchup

Use store-bought bread crumbs for super-fast nuggets.

What to do

1 Grate the bread. Put the crumbs into a shallow bowl and *season*. *Beat* the eggs. Pour them into another shallow bowl.

2 Flatten the chicken breasts with your hands, then carefully cut them into chunks about 1 in (2½ cm) across.

3 Dip the chicken pieces into the egg and turn them to coat on all sides. Then coat them in the bread crumbs.

4 Heat the oil in a frying pan and *fry* the nuggets for about 10 minutes, turning them until they are brown on all sides.

LEMONY FISH STICKS

You will need

Cutting board • Sharp knife • Grater
or food processor • Grater or zester
Bowl • Whisk or fork • 2 shallow bowls
Frying pan • Spatula

Ingredients

 Small bunch parsley

2 slices stale bread

1 lemon

Salt and pepper

2 eggs

1 lb (450 g) skinned and
boned white fish fillets

1 tablespoon
vegetable oil

 Pat of butter

Tasty tips

If you like dried mixed herbs,
add a small pinch to the
bread crumbs in step 1.

What to do

1 *Chop* the parsley. Grate the bread. Peel or grate the zest from the lemon, then mix the 3 ingredients in a bowl and *season*.

2 *Beat* the eggs. Put the eggs and the bread crumbs into two separate shallow bowls. Cut the fish into stick shapes.

3 Dip the pieces of fish in the beaten egg and then in the bread crumbs. Make sure each fish stick is coated evenly.

4 Heat the oil and butter in a frying pan. *Fry* the fish sticks for about 4 minutes on each side until crisp and golden.

BARBECUED SPARE RIBS

You will need

Garlic press • Bowl • Whisk or fork
Shallow dish • Broiler pan (if using
broiler) • Tongs • Pastry brush
Small saucepan • Wooden spoon

Ingredients

12 pork
spare ribs

For the barbecue sauce

 1 clove garlic

 2 tablespoons
dark brown sugar

2 tablespoons light
soy sauce

 2 tablespoons
tomato paste

1 tablespoon
maple syrup or honey

½ teaspoon prepared mustard

Black pepper

What to do

1 Crush the garlic. Put it in
a bowl with the sugar, soy
sauce, tomato paste, maple syrup,
mustard, and pepper. Whisk well.

2 Lay the ribs in a shallow
dish. Pour the sauce over
the ribs, then let them *marinate*
for at least 20 minutes.

3 Heat the broiler or barbecue
until hot. *Grill* the ribs for
about 15 minutes on each side.
Brush with sauce if needed.

4 Heat any sauce that is left
over in a saucepan, let it
simmer and serve it with the
barbecued spare ribs.

*Each rib is
coated with
delicious
barbecue
sauce.*

VEGETABLE BARBECUE

You will need

Cutting board • Skewers • Small bowl • Pastry brush • Broiler pan (if using broiler) • Tongs • Metal skewer (for testing) • Sharp knife

Ingredients

20 cherry tomatoes

2 ears of corn

Olive oil

Salt and pepper

Tasty tips

You can either grill or barbecue the vegetables. They go well with the barbecued spare ribs on page 40, or with salads and bread.

What to do

1 Heat the broiler or barbecue. Thread the tomatoes onto skewers. Brush the corn with olive oil, then *season* it.

2 *Grill* the tomatoes and corn, turning them so they cook evenly. The tomatoes will take about 5 minutes.

3 When the corn is golden brown, push a skewer into it to see if it is tender. It should take 5 to 10 minutes to cook.

4 Leave the cooked corn until it is cool enough to handle, then carefully cut it into chunks about 1½ in (4 cm) wide.

Barbecued corn

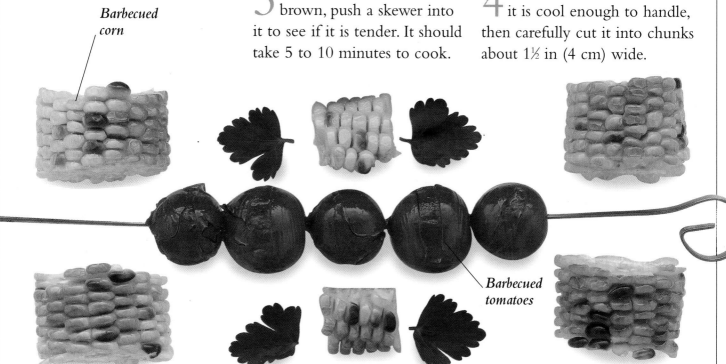

Barbecued tomatoes

41

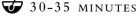

CHICKEN CHOW MEIN

You will need

Large saucepan • Wooden spoon
Colander • Cutting board
Vegetable peeler • Sharp knife
Grater • Garlic press • Large frying
pan or wok • Lemon squeezer

For the noodles

 8 oz (225 g) dried medium egg noodles

 1 teaspoon sunflower oil

For the stir-fry

2 carrots

¼ lb (115 g) thin green beans

¼ lb (115 g) snow peas

4 scallions

1 in (2½ cm) piece fresh ginger

1 clove garlic

 2 tablespoons sunflower oil

2 skinless chicken breasts

 1 tablespoon soy sauce

½ lemon

½ teaspoon salt

Tasty tips

• For a change, try steak or pork fillet instead of chicken.

• For vegetarian chow mein, replace the chicken with 2 zucchini and half a head of broccoli.

What to do

1 Half-fill a large saucepan with water and bring it to a *boil*. Add the noodles and *boil* them for 4 minutes.

2 Drain the noodles in a colander and rinse them in cold water. Return them to the pan and mix in the sunflower oil.

3 Peel the carrots and cut them into thin sticks. Trim the beans and snow peas. Trim and *slice* the scallions.

4 Peel the ginger and grate it coarsely. Peel the garlic and either crush it with a garlic press or chop it finely.

5 Heat the oil in a frying pan. Cut the chicken into strips, *stir-fry* it for a few minutes until golden, then leave it on a plate.

6 Put the garlic, ginger, carrots, and beans in the frying pan. *Stir-fry* them for 4 to 5 minutes, turning them all the time.

7 Add the chicken, snow peas, scallions, and noodles. Mix everything together and cook for a few more minutes.

8 Add the soy sauce, the juice of half a lemon, and the salt and mix once more. Cook for 2 minutes to heat through.

Soy sauce

Noodle feast

Chow mein is noodles *stir-fried* with lots of tasty vegetables. Try using chopsticks to eat it like the Chinese do!

Chopsticks

CHICKEN CURRY AND RICE

You will need

Cutting board • Sharp knife
Grater • Large frying pan
with lid • Wooden spoon
Plate • Saucepan with lid

For the chicken curry

 1 in (2½ cm) piece fresh ginger

1 onion

 2 cloves garlic

4 skinless
chicken breasts

2 tablespoons vegetable oil

 2 tablespoons mild
curry powder

1 cup (200 ml)
chicken stock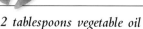

Salt and pepper

4 tablespoons
plain yogurt

1 sprig fresh coriander

For the rice

 1 small onion

2 tablespoons butter

1 stick cinnamon

1 teaspoon ground turmeric

 ¼ cup (225 g)
long grain rice

Salt

 2½ cups (600 ml)
chicken or vegetable stock

Making the chicken curry

1 Cut the peel off the piece of ginger with a sharp knife, then grate the ginger on the coarsest part of the grater.

2 Peel the onion and the garlic, then *chop* them both finely. Carefully cut the chicken into bite-sized pieces.

3 Heat the oil in a frying pan. When hot, cook the chicken pieces quickly on all sides until golden, then move them to a plate.

4 *Fry* the onion and garlic until they turn brown at the edges. Stir in the ginger and curry powder and cook for 1 minute.

5 Add the chicken, then the stock. Put the lid on the frying pan and cook over low heat for about 20 minutes.

6 Let the curry cool for a few minutes, then stir in the *seasoning* and yogurt. *Chop* the coriander and add it to the curry.

Making the rice

1 *Chop* the onion finely. Melt the butter in a pan and cook the onion until soft. Add the spices, and cook for 1 minute.

2 Add the rice and salt and stir well. Cook over low heat for a few more minutes until the rice looks transparent.

3 Pour in the stock. Put a lid on the pan and *simmer* for 15 to 20 minutes until the rice is tender and has absorbed the stock.

Curry feast

Spread the rice out on a warm serving plate and spoon the chicken curry on top.

THAI KEBABS WITH SATAY SAUCE

You will need

Bamboo skewers • Cutting board
Sharp knife • Bowl • Garlic press
Grater • Whisk • 3 shallow bowls
Saucepan • Wooden spoon • Broiler pan

For the kebabs

 1 small pork fillet

2 small skinless chicken breasts

 12 large cooked, peeled shrimp

For the marinade

 2 tablespoons soy sauce

2 tablespoons honey

Juice of 1 lime

A few drops Tabasco sauce

 1 clove garlic

½ in (1 cm) piece fresh ginger

For the satay sauce

 ½ onion

½ in (1 cm) piece fresh ginger

 1 clove garlic

1½ tablespoons vegetable oil

1½ teaspoons soy sauce

3 tablespoons water

 1½ tablespoons light brown sugar

5 tablespoons peanut butter

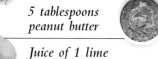 Juice of 1 lime

Salt if needed

Preparing the meat

1 Soak the skewers in water for 30 minutes. Cut the pork into thin diagonal slices, then cut each slice into narrow strips.

2 Flatten the chicken breasts with your hands, then carefully cut them into strips about 1 in (2½ cm) wide.

Making the marinade

1 Put the soy sauce, honey, lime juice, and Tabasco into a bowl. Crush the garlic, peel and grate the ginger, and stir them in.

2 Pour the marinade into 3 bowls. Put the pork, chicken, and shrimp into the 3 bowls, turn them, and let *marinate*.

Making the satay sauce

1 Peel the onion and *chop* it very finely. Peel the ginger and grate it coarsely, then peel and crush the garlic.

2 Heat the oil in a saucepan. Cook the onion gently until soft. Add the ginger and garlic and cook for a few minutes.

Making the kebabs

3 Put the onion mixture, soy sauce, water, sugar, peanut butter, and lime juice in a bowl and whisk. Add salt if needed.

1 Thread the shrimp onto skewers. Fold the strips of pork and chicken and thread them onto separate skewers.

2 *Grill* the pork and chicken for about 4 minutes on each side until brown. *Grill* the shrimp for about 1 minute on each side.

Thai treat

Serve the kebabs with wedges of fresh lime and a bowl of satay sauce.

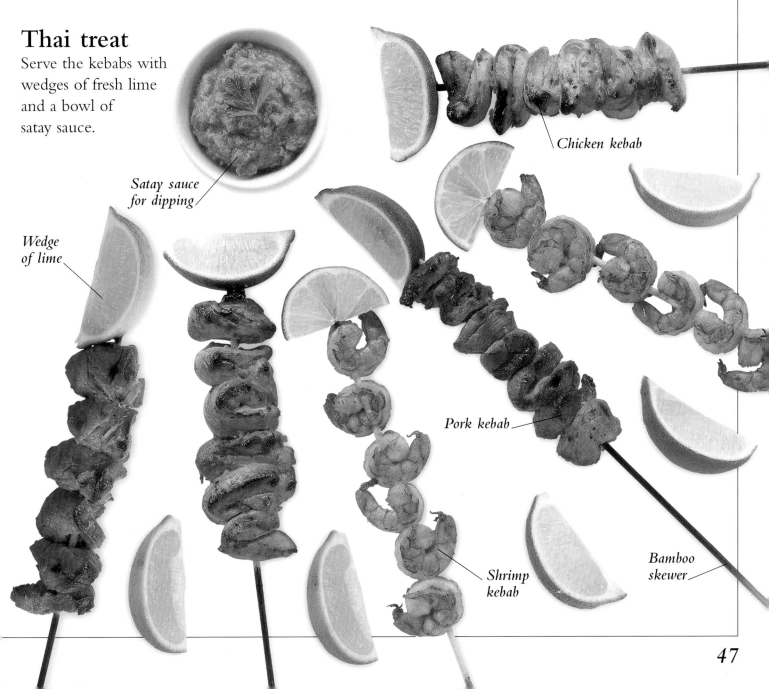

Satay sauce for dipping

Chicken kebab

Wedge of lime

Pork kebab

Shrimp kebab

Bamboo skewer

47

SALADE NIÇOISE

You will need

Cutting board • Vegetable peeler
Sharp knife • 3 saucepans
Colander or sieve • Bowl • Dish towel
Screw-top jar • Salad bowl

For the salad

1 large potato

¼ lb (115 g) green beans

3 eggs

6 medium tomatoes

3 scallions

1 bunch parsley

1 head iceberg lettuce

14 oz (400 g) canned tuna fish

6 anchovy fillets

¾ cup (85 g) pitted black olives

For the dressing

3 tablespoons olive oil

1 tablespoon wine vinegar

½ teaspoon French mustard

Salt and pepper

What to do

1 Peel the potato and cut it into bite-sized chunks. *Boil* the potato until tender, drain it, and let cool.

2 Trim the beans, then cook them in a saucepan of *boiling* water for 5 minutes until tender. Rinse them under cold water.

3 *Boil* the eggs for 10 minutes, then put them in a bowl of cold water to cool. Peel the eggs and cut them into quarters.

4 Cut up the tomatoes. Rinse and dry the parsley, cut off the stalks, and *chop* the leaves finely. *Slice* the scallions.

5 Put the olive oil, vinegar, mustard, salt, and pepper into a jar. Screw on the lid and shake well to make the dressing.

6 Rinse the lettuce leaves in a bowl of cold water. Drain them, then pat them dry. Line a salad bowl with the leaves.

7 Arrange the potatoes, tuna, tomatoes, scallions, beans, eggs, and parsley on top of the lettuce and sprinkle with dressing.

8 Drain the anchovies and cut them in half lengthwise. Lay them on top of the salad and garnish with the olives.

Extra dressing

Mouthwatering salad

To make a light meal, serve the salad with warm, crusty French bread. Pour any leftover salad dressing into a small pitcher and serve it separately.

Arrange the anchovies in a crisscross pattern.

TABBOULEH

You will need

2 large bowls • Cutting board
Sharp knife • Dish towel
Large sieve • Salad bowl
Wooden spoon

Ingredients

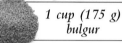 1 cup (175 g) bulgur

½ cucumber

4 scallions

1 bunch parsley

Small handful mint leaves

 3 tablespoons olive oil

 3 tablespoons lemon juice

Salt and pepper

Tasty tips

For extra color, add 3 seeded, diced tomatoes and a handful of pitted black olives.

What to do

1 Put the bulgur in a bowl, cover it with *boiling* water, and let soak for 20 minutes until the grains soften.

2 Finely *chop* the cucumber. Trim the scallions and *slice* them finely. Rinse, dry, and finely *chop* the parsley and mint.

3 Drain the bulgur in a sieve over a bowl. Use your hands to squeeze out as much extra water as you can.

4 Put all the ingredients for the tabbouleh into a salad bowl. Mix everything together and *season* with salt and pepper.

Garnish the tabbouleh with sprigs of mint and serve it with slices of lemon.

CARROT SALAD

You will need

Cutting board • Kitchen brush or vegetable peeler • Grater • Cookie sheet Lemon squeezer • Small jar with lid Salad bowl with servers

For the salad

 6 large carrots

 1 tablespoon sunflower seeds

 ½ cup (85 g) raisins

For the dressing

 ½ orange

 ½ lemon

 1 teaspoon honey

 3 tablespoons hazelnut or olive oil

¼ teaspoon prepared French mustard

Salt and pepper

Decorate the salad by sprinkling a few extra raisins and sunflower seeds over the top.

What to do

1 Scrub or peel the carrots and grate them coarsely. Toast the sunflower seeds lightly under the broiler for a few minutes.

2 Squeeze the juice out of the orange and lemon. Put the dressing ingredients into a jar, screw on the lid, and shake well.

3 Put the carrot, sunflower seeds, and raisins into a salad bowl. Pour the dressing over the top and toss the salad.

FILLED CREPES

You will need

Bowl • Whisk • Measuring cup
Small frying pan • Pastry
brush • Spatula • Warm plate
Cutting board • Grater
Sharp knife • Wooden spoon • Spoon

For the crepes

½ cup (55 g)
all-purpose flour

½ cup (55 g)
whole-wheat flour

Pinch of salt

2 eggs

1 cup (200 ml) milk

½ cup (100 ml) water

4 tablespoons melted butter

Cheesy filling

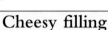

½ lb (225 g)
Gruyère cheese

½ lb (225 g) smoked ham

Mushroom filling

½ lb (225 g) mushrooms

4 tablespoons butter

Pinch of flour

Pinch of grated nutmeg

Salt and pepper

4 tablespoons heavy
or sour cream

What to do

1 Put all the flour and salt in a bowl. Add the eggs and some of the milk and water, whisking them in a little bit at a time.

2 Gradually pour the rest of the milk and water into the mixture, whisking until everything is mixed evenly.

3 Add half the melted butter to the mixture and whisk it again to make the finished batter. Pour it into a measuring cup.

4 Brush a frying pan with melted butter and heat until it sizzles. Then pour in 2 tablespoons of crepe batter.

5 Quickly tilt the pan from side to side, so that the bottom of the pan is covered completely with a thin layer of batter.

6 Cook the crepe for about 1 minute, then flip it over and cook it for 10 more seconds. Slide it onto a warm plate.

Cheesy filling

Grate the cheese and *dice* the ham, then mix them together. Sprinkle some of the mixture onto each crepe and fold it over.

Mushroom filling

1 Wipe and finely chop the mushrooms. Melt the butter in a pan and *fry* the mushrooms for a few minutes until tender.

2 Add the flour and *seasoning*. Stir for a minute, then add the cream. Spoon a little filling onto each crepe and fold it over.

Savor the flavor

These filled crepes make a delicious light lunch or snack.

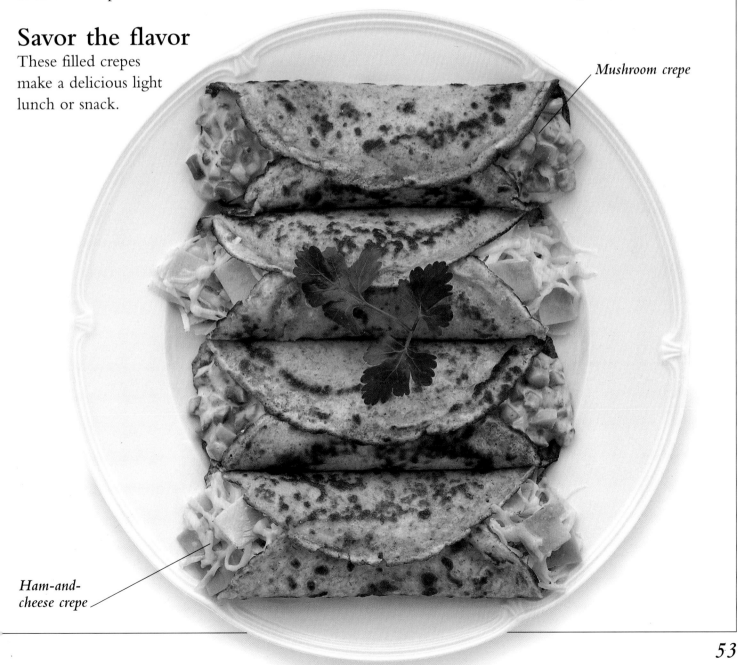

Mushroom crepe

Ham-and-cheese crepe

53

SPICY CHICKEN BURGERS

You will need

Cutting board
Sharp knife • Plastic bag
Frying pan • Spatula
Bread knife • Spoon

For the chicken filling

2 large, skinless
chicken breasts

½ cup (55 g)
all-purppose flour

¼ teaspoon chili powder

Salt and pepper

Vegetable oil for frying

For the burgers

4 sesame-seed
hamburger buns

Shredded lettuce

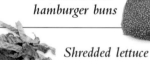

Sour cream

Prepared salsa
or sliced tomato

What to do

1 Carefully cut the chicken breasts in half. Flatten them out by pressing them firmly with the palm of your hand.

2 Put the flour, chili powder, salt, pepper, and chicken in a plastic bag. Fold over the top of the bag and shake it well.

3 Heat the oil in a frying pan until hot. *Fry* the chicken for about 8 minutes on each side until firm and golden brown.

4 Cut the rolls in half. Fill each one with lettuce, a piece of chicken, sour cream, and salsa or sliced tomato.

Nice spice

Chili powder and sour cream give these burgers a great Tex–Mex flavor.

Salsa

Sour cream

Spicy chicken

Shredded lettuce

Sliced tomato

DELIGHTFUL DESSERTS

CREAM PUFFS

You will need

Cookie sheet • Sharp knife • Saucepan
Sieve • Waxed paper • Wooden spoon
Whisk or fork • 2 teaspoons • Wire rack
Bowl • Whisk or electric mixer

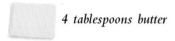

For the cream puffs

Butter for greasing cookie sheet

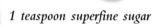

4 tablespoons butter

½ cup (125 ml) water

½ cup (70 g)
all-purpose flour

1 teaspoon superfine sugar

2 eggs

For the sauce

4 oz (115 g)
semisweet chocolate

2 tablespoons butter

4 tablespoons heavy cream

For the filling

⅔ cup (150 ml)
heavy cream

Tasty tips

You can use this recipe to make
chocolate éclairs. Fill a piping bag
with the cream-puff mixture and
pipe short fingers on a cookie sheet.
Bake in the same way as the cream
puffs. Fill with whipped cream
and top with chocolate sauce.

What to do

1 Set the oven. *Grease* a cookie
sheet and dampen it with
water. Cut up the butter and heat
it in a saucepan with the water.

2 *Sift* the flour and sugar onto
waxed paper. When the
water *boils*, remove it from the
heat and add the flour and sugar.

3 *Beat* the mixture hard with
a wooden spoon until it is
smooth and comes away from
the sides of the saucepan.

4 *Beat* the eggs, then *beat* them
into the mixture, a little at a
time, until you have a thick,
smooth, glossy paste.

5 Put teaspoons of the mixture
onto the cookie sheet. *Bake*
for 20 to 25 minutes until puffy
and golden brown.

6 Put the cream puffs on a wire
rack to cool. Pierce them with
a fork to let out any steam and to
keep them from getting soft.

7 Break the chocolate into a saucepan. Add the butter and cream. Stir over low heat until the chocolate has melted.

8 Whip the cream for the filling in a bowl until thick. Slice open each puff and fill with the cream.

9 Arrange the profiteroles on a serving plate. Pour over the chocolate sauce, making sure each cream puff is lightly coated.

Chocolate feast

Pour any extra chocolate sauce into a small pitcher and serve it with the cream puffs.

Eat the cream puffs as soon as you can – they taste best when they're fresh.

BAKED ALASKA

You will need

Cookie sheet • Spoon or knife
Big spoon or ice-cream scoop
Butter knife • Mixing bowl
Whisk or electric mixer

Ingredients

 8 in (20 cm) cake flan case or 6-7 slices of sponge cake

 2 tablespoons strawberry jam

1 pint (500 ml) strawberry ice cream

3 egg whites

Pinch of salt

¾ cup (175 g) superfine sugar

Tasty tips

Instead of using jam you could cover the sponge cake with sliced strawberries or other fresh fruit. You can use ice cream in any flavor you like.

What to do

1 Preheat oven. Put the cake flan case or slices of sponge cake on the cookie sheet and spread the jam evenly on top.

2 Scoop the ice cream onto the cake and smooth it into a rounded shape with a knife. Put it in the freezer until needed.

3 Put the egg whites and salt in a bowl and *whisk* them until they form stiff peaks. Whisk in the sugar, a little at a time.

4 Quickly cover the flan case and ice cream with the egg white. *Bake* for 3 to 5 minutes until the meringue is pale golden.

Make peaks in the meringue before cooking it.

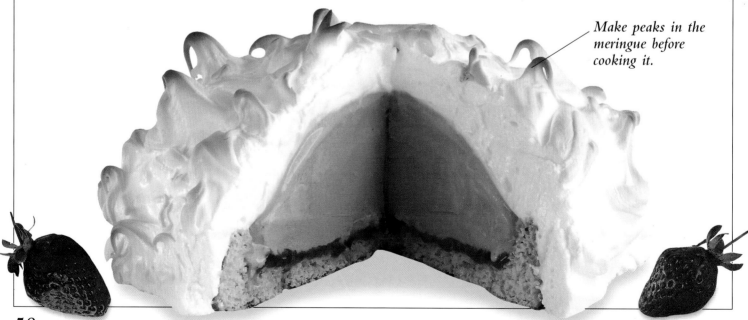

KNICKERBOCKER GLORIES

You will need

Cutting board • Sharp knife
Tall glass • Spoon or ice-cream scoop
Spoon or piping bag
Long-handled spoon

For the strawberry glory

 6 large strawberries

3 scoops
strawberry ice cream

Strawberry-flavored syrup

 1 tablespoon
whipped cream

½ tablespoon toasted
sliced almonds

For the banana glory

 1 banana

3 scoops butter pecan or
butterscotch ice cream

Maple syrup

 1 tablespoon
whipped cream

½ tablespoon chopped
pecans or walnuts

Serve each glory with
a long-handled spoon

Strawberry
glory

Banana
glory

What to do

1 Hull, wash, and dry the strawberries. Slice the fruit. If making a banana glory, peel and slice the banana.

2 Put layers of ice cream and sliced fruit in a tall glass. When the glass is nearly full, pour a little syrup over the top.

3 Pipe or spoon whipped cream on top of the ice cream and fruit, then sprinkle with the nuts.

LEMON CHEESECAKE

You will need

Plastic bag • Rolling pin • Saucepan
Wooden spoon • 8 in (20 cm)
cake pan (preferably spring form)
Grater or zester • Lemon squeezer
2 large bowls • Whisk or electric mixer
Metal spoon • Plate

For the base

Graham crackers or plain cookies to make 3 cups (175 g) of crumbs.

 5 tablespoons butter

Butter for greasing cake pan

For the filling

1 lemon

2 eggs

1½ cups (340 g) mascarpone or other cream cheese

½ cup (115 g) fromage frais or sour cream

Scant ½ cup (85 g) superfine sugar

1 tablespoon cornstarch

For the decoration

Strips of orange and lemon zest

Tasty tips

Orange cheesecake is also delicious and easy to make. Just replace the lemon zest and lemon juice with the grated zest and juice of an orange.

What to do

1 Preheat the oven. Break the cookies into a large plastic bag and crush them with a rolling pin to make them into crumbs.

2 Melt the butter in a saucepan over low heat. Turn off the heat and stir the cookie crumbs into the butter.

3 *Grease* the cake pan. Add the cookie crumbs and press them down evenly to make a base. Now make the filling.

4 Grate the zest from the lemon. Cut the lemon in half and squeeze out the juice. *Separate* the eggs into two bowls.

5 Whisk the lemon zest, lemon juice, egg yolks, mascarpone, fromage frais, sugar, and cornstarch in a bowl until smooth.

6 Wash and dry the whisk or electric mixer, then *whisk* the egg whites in a separate bowl until they are stiff and form peaks.

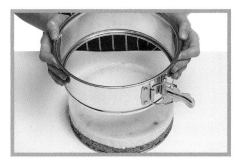

7 Add the whisked egg whites to the cheese mixture. *Fold* them in gently with a metal spoon until they are well mixed.

8 Spoon the filling onto the base and *bake* for 50 minutes. Turn off the oven and let the cheesecake cool in the oven.

9 Take the cheesecake out of the oven, remove it from the pan, and put it on a plate. Chill it in the refrigerator overnight.

Tangy cheesecake

Lemon cheesecake is so delicious and rich, it is best served on its own.

Decorate the cheesecake with fine strips of orange and lemon zest.

TIRAMISU

You will need

Grater or food processor
Mixing bowl • Whisk • Shallow dish
4 individual glasses or 1 glass serving
bowl • Spoon • Teaspoon

Ingredients

2 oz (55 g)
dark chocolate

1 cup (225 g) mascarpone

1 cup (225 g) fromage
frais or sour cream

¼ cup (55 g) superfine
sugar

¼ cup (300 ml)
strong coffee

20 sponge fingers
or lady fingers

What to do

1 Grate the chocolate with a grater or in a food processor. Whisk the mascarpone, fromage frais, and the sugar together.

2 Pour the coffee into a dish. Break the sponge fingers in half, dip them in the coffee, and put a layer in each glass.

3 Cover the sponge fingers with a layer of cream cheese and sprinkle with a little of the grated chocolate.

4 Repeat the layers, finishing with cream cheese. Sprinkle this with chocolate and chill in the refrigerator for 2 to 3 hours.

*Chilling the tiramisu
helps blend the flavors
of the coffee, cream cheese,
and chocolate.*

CLAFOUTI

You will need

9 in (23 cm) ovenproof dish or ceramic flan dish • Cutting board Sharp knife • Saucepan • Mixing bowl • Wooden spoon or whisk Small sieve or tea strainer

Ingredients

Butter for greasing ovenproof dish

1¼ lb (565 g) prune plums

3 tablespoons butter

3 large eggs

½ cup (85 g) superfine sugar

⅔ cup (100 ml) light cream

⅓ cup (85 g) all-purpose flour or ground almonds

Confectioners' sugar

Tasty tips

You can also make clafouti with cherries, apricots, apples, peaches, or pears.

What to do

1 Preheat the oven and *grease* an ovenproof dish. Cut the plums in half and *pit* them. Cut each plum half in two.

2 Melt the butter in a pan. In a bowl, *beat* together the melted butter, eggs, sugar, cream, and flour or ground almonds.

3 Pour the mixture into the ovenproof dish and arrange the quartered plums in a pretty pattern in it.

4 Cook the clafouti for 40 to 45 minutes until set in the center. Let it cool a little, then sprinkle with confectioners' sugar.

Clafouti is delicious when it has cooled a little but is still warm. Serve it with whipped cream.

FRUIT CRUMBLE

You will need

Pie pan • Cutting board • Vegetable peeler • Sharp knife • Saucepan Wooden spoon • Mixing bowl • Spoon

For the filling

Butter for greasing

 1½ lb (675 g) cooking apples

2 tablespoons (30 g) soft brown sugar

1 teaspoon cinnamon

2 tablespoons apple juice

 1 cup (225 g) blackberries

For the crumble

½ cup (120 g) butter

1½ cups all-purpose or whole-wheat flour

½ cup (55 g) oatmeal

½ cup (85 g) light brown sugar

Pinch of salt

Tasty tips

You can use apricots, plums, or raspberries instead of blackberries in the crumble.

What to do

1 Preheat the oven. *Grease* the pie pan. Peel the apples, cut them into quarters, and cut out the cores, then slice them.

2 Cook the apples, sugar, cinnamon, and apple juice gently in a saucepan until the apples are soft, but not pulpy.

3 Meanwhile *cut* the butter and flour together in a mixing bowl, then mix in the oats, sugar, and salt.

4 Put the apples into the dish and mix in the blackberries. Spread the crumble on top and *bake* for 30 to 40 minutes.

You can serve fruit crumble hot or cold. It is delicious with a scoop of vanilla ice cream.

FRUIT SALAD

You will need

Cutting board • Sharp knife
Glass or white china bowl
Large spoon

Ingredients

1 lb (450 g) fresh or canned pineapple rings

Half a fresh melon

Medium bunch seedless grapes

Half a mango or small can of sliced peaches

½ cup (100 ml) pineapple juice

Tasty tips

You can make fruit salad with any fruit you like: try strawberries, raspberries, cherries, and sliced banana.

Decorate the fruit salad with a sprig of mint.

What to do

1 Cut up the pineapple. Cut the melon into slices, remove the seeds and skin, and then cut the slices into chunks.

2 Wash the grapes and cut them in half. Score the flesh of the mango as shown, then slice the chunks away from the skin.

3 Put all the fruit in the bowl, pour the pineapple juice on top, and stir everything together. Chill until needed.

HOT CHOCOLATE SOUFFLÉS

You will need

*3 bowls • Saucepan
Wooden spoon • 4 ramekins • Whisk
or electric mixer • Large metal spoon
Small sieve or tea strainer*

Ingredients

 4 oz (115 g) fine dark chocolate

Butter for greasing ramekins

Scant ½ cup (55 g) superfine sugar

5 eggs

Pinch of salt

Confectioners' sugar

What to do

1 Set the oven. Break the chocolate into a bowl. Melt it over a saucepan of *simmering* water, stirring until smooth.

2 Remove the chocolate from the heat. *Grease* the four ramekins lightly and sprinkle with a little of the superfine sugar.

3 *Separate* the eggs into two bowls. Stir the rest of the superfine sugar and four egg yolks into the melted chocolate.

4 *Whisk* all five egg whites with a pinch of salt until they form stiff peaks. Then *fold* them gently into the chocolate.

5 Fill the ramekins until nearly full. *Bake* for 15 minutes until they rise and puff up. Sprinkle with confectioners' sugar.

Serve the soufflés right away.

RASPBERRY FOOLS

You will need

2 bowls • Fork • Large spoon
Whisk or electric mixer • 4 ramekins

Ingredients

 ½ pint (285 g) raspberries

1 teaspoon lemon juice

2 tablespoons superfine sugar

⅔ cup (150 ml) heavy cream

Generous ½ cup (140 g) sour cream

Tasty tips

Try making the fool with other types of soft fruit. Leave out the lemon juice and sugar. Once you have made the fool, taste it and add sugar if necessary.

What to do

1 Set aside eight raspberries. Crush the rest with a fork, leaving them a little lumpy. Stir in the lemon juice and sugar.

2 Pour the heavy cream into another bowl and *beat* it with a whisk or electric mixer until it has thickened.

Keep the fools chilled until you are ready to serve them.

3 *Fold* the sour cream and the cream gently into the raspberries, then spoon the fool into the four ramekins.

Decorate the fools with the remaining whole raspberries.

TOTALLY TERRIFIC TRIFLE

You will need
Glass bowl • Spoon • Saucepan
Wooden spoon • Bowl • Whisk or fork
Cutting board • Knife • Colander
Whisk or electric mixer • Butter knife

For the trifle

 Slices of sponge cake or 5 large macaroons

 Apricot or raspberry jam

 5 tablespoons fruit juice or syrup

2 firm, ripe bananas

 14 oz (400 g) canned sliced peaches

For the custard

1¼ cups (300 ml) heavy cream

1 teaspoon cornstarch

3 egg yolks

Few drops vanilla extract (optional)

 2 tablespoons superfine sugar

For the topping

1¼ cups (300 ml) heavy cream

 ¼ cup (30 g) toasted flaked almonds

Handy hints
For a super-speedy trifle, instead of preparing the custard from scratch, mix up a package of instant custard or vanilla pudding.

What to do

1 Break the slices of sponge cake or macaroons into medium-sized pieces and lay them in the bottom of the bowl.

2 Spread a thin layer of jam over the top of the cake pieces or macaroons, then spoon on enough fruit juice or syrup to soak them.

3 Put the cream for the custard in a saucepan and heat gently until it boils. Beat the cornstarch, eggs, vanilla, and sugar in a bowl.

4 As soon as the cream boils, stir it into the egg mixture a little at a time. Keep stirring the mixture to stop it from curdling.

5 Return the mixture to the pan and stir it over very low heat until it thickens. Remove from the heat and let cool.

6 Peel and slice the bananas and arrange them on top of the jam, then drain the peaches and lay them on top of the bananas.

7 When the custard has cooled completely, carefully spoon it over the layer of peaches, making sure it is spread out evenly.

8 Whip the heavy cream for the topping with a whisk or electric mixer until it is thick but not completely stiff.

9 Spread the whipped cream over the custard with a butter knife and decorate it with flaked almonds.

Tempting trifle

Creamy, fruity trifle is a good dessert for a party, summer barbecue, or other special occasion.

Decorate the trifle with fresh raspberries.

FRUITY CRÈME BRÛLÉES

You will need

Cutting board • Sharp knife
4 ramekins • Spoon • Knife
Cookie sheet or broiler pan

Ingredients

 Small bunch of seedless grapes

1 pint (175 g) strawberries

1 cup (250 g) plain yogurt

¾ cup (175 g) soft brown sugar or superfine sugar

Tasty tips

You can make these tasty treats with all sorts of fruit: try sliced banana, mandarin segments, or your favorite berries.

What to do

1 Wash the grapes and cut them in half. Hull, wash, and dry the strawberries, then half-fill the ramekins with fruit.

2 Turn the broiler onto a high setting. Cover the fruit with yogurt, then smooth the top of the yogurt flat with a knife.

3 Sprinkle enough soft brown sugar on top of the yogurt to completely cover it. It should be at least ¼ in (½ cm) thick.

4 Stand the ramekins on a cookie sheet and put them under the hot broiler for a few minutes until the sugar caramelizes.

Beneath the crunchy caramel topping is a creamy mixture of fruit and yogurt.

TREATS
AND
SWEETS

ULTIMATE CHOCOLATE CAKE

You will need

8 in (20 cm) cake pan with loose base
Waxed paper • Bowl • Saucepan
Wooden spoon • Knife • 2 large bowls
Whisk or electric mixer • Sieve
Metal spoon • Wire rack • Butter knife

For the cake

Butter for greasing cake pan

 6 oz (175 g) dark chocolate

8 tablespoons butter

3 tablespoons water

 3 eggs

 ⅔ cup (140 g) superfine sugar

 ¾ cup (85 g) ground almonds

½ cup (55 g) self-rising flour

Pinch of salt

For the icing

4 oz (115 g) dark chocolate

2 tablespoons sour cream

For the decoration

 Sliced almonds

Tasty tips

• Instead of plain sliced almonds, you could use toasted ones for extra flavor.

• You could decorate the cake with fresh strawberry halves.

Making the cake

1 Set the oven. *Grease* the cake pan, then cut out a circle of waxed paper and *line* the bottom of the pan with it.

2 Break the chocolate into a bowl. Stand it over a saucepan of *simmering* water and stir until all the chocolate has melted.

3 Cut the butter into small pieces. Add the butter and water to the chocolate and stir until the butter has melted.

4 *Separate* the eggs into two large bowls. *Beat* the egg yolks and sugar together until they are thick and creamy.

5 Stir the chocolate mixture into the egg yolk mixture. Add the ground almonds, *sift* in the flour, and mix well.

6 *Whisk* the egg whites with a pinch of salt until they form stiff peaks. *Fold* them gently into the chocolate mixture.

Making the icing

7 Put the mixture into the pan. *Bake* for 40 to 45 minutes. Cool in the pan for 5 minutes, then move to a wire rack.

1 Melt the chocolate in a bowl over a pan of *simmering* water. Remove from the heat and stir in the sour cream.

2 Spread the chocolate icing over the top of the cooled cake with a butter knife, then decorate it with sliced almonds.

Scrumptious cake

When this cake comes out of the oven, it has a gooey chocolate center that sets as it cools.

FROSTED CARROT CAKE

You will need

8 in (20 cm) round cake pan
Waxed paper • Sharp knife • Grater
or food processor • Sieve • Large bowl
Wooden spoon • Whisk or fork • Bowl
Spoon • Skewer • Wire rack • Butter knife

For the cake

Butter for greasing cake pan

4 large carrots

*2 cups (225 g) flour
and 5 teaspoons
baking powder*

Pinch of salt

 *⅔ cup (140 g)
soft brown sugar*

Grated zest of 1 orange

2 teaspoons ground cinnamon

*1 cup (115 g) chopped
roasted hazelnuts
or chopped walnuts*

½ cup (55 g) dried coconut

2 large eggs

*⅔ cup (150 ml)
sunflower oil*

Juice of 1 orange

For the frosting

 *8 oz (225 g)
cream cheese*

6 tablespoons (85 g) butter

 *1 cup (115 g)
confectioners' sugar*

For the marzipan carrots

 8 oz (225 g) marzipan

Orange and green food coloring

Making the cake

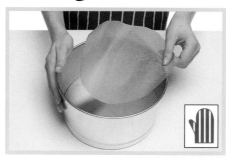

1 Preheat the oven. *Grease* the cake pan. Cut out a circle of waxed paper the same size as the pan and cover the base with it.

2 Scrub or peel the carrots and trim off their tops. Grate the carrots using a grater or a food processor.

3 *Sift* the flour and baking powder into a bowl. Mix in the carrots, salt, sugar, orange zest, cinnamon, nuts, and coconut.

4 *Beat* the eggs. Add the eggs, sunflower oil, and orange juice to the cake mixture and mix everything together well.

5 Spoon the mixture into the cake pan. *Bake* it for 60 to 75 minutes until a skewer pushed into the center comes out clean.

6 Let the cake cool in the pan for 10 to 15 minutes, then remove it from the pan and put it on a wire rack to finish cooling.

Decorating the cake

1 *Beat* the cream cheese, butter, and confectioners' sugar in a bowl with a wooden spoon until the mixture is soft and creamy.

2 Spread the cream-cheese frosting evenly over the top of the cooled cake, using a butter knife dipped in warm water.

3 Knead orange and green food coloring into two balls of marzipan, then mold carrots for the top of the cake.

Snacking special

Spicy carrot cake will stay fresh for several days if you store it in an airtight container.

Use a fork to make decorative swirls in the frosting.

MACAROONS

You will need

Cookie sheet • Waxed paper
2 bowls • Whisk or electric mixer
Metal spoon • Wire rack

Ingredients

 2 eggs

1½ cups (175 g)
ground almonds

¾ cup (175 g)
superfine sugar

What to do

1 Preheat oven. Line a cookie sheet with waxed paper. *Separate* the egg whites from the yolks and put them in two bowls.

2 Put the yolks in the refrigerator, you will not need them. *Whisk* the egg whites until they form stiff peaks.

3 Add the ground almonds and sugar to the egg whites and *fold* them in gently with a metal spoon until well mixed.

4 Roll the mixture into small balls, then put the balls on the cookie sheet. *Bake* them for 15 minutes until golden brown.

5 Take the macaroons out of the oven and cool them on a wire rack. Store the macaroons in an airtight container.

Macaroons crack naturally as they cook.

These cookies are very light and seem to melt in the mouth.

CHOCOLATE MACAROONS

You will need

Cookie sheet • Waxed paper
3 bowls • Saucepan • Wooden spoon
Whisk or electric mixer • Metal
spoon • Teaspoon • Wire rack

Ingredients

2 medium eggs

3 oz (85 g)
semisweet chocolate

1½ cups (175 g)
ground almonds

½ cup (115 g)
superfine sugar

What to do

1 Preheat the oven. Line a cookie sheet with waxed paper. *Separate* the eggs and put them in two different bowls.

2 Break the chocolate into a bowl and heat it over a pan of *simmering* water until it melts. Stir the chocolate until smooth.

3 *Whisk* the egg whites until stiff, then *fold* the almonds, sugar, and egg whites into the chocolate until mixed together.

4 Put teaspoons of the mixture onto the cookie sheet. *Bake* for 15 to 20 minutes, then move to a wire rack to cool.

Once the macaroons have cooled, store them in an airtight container to keep them crisp.

77

OAT BARS

You will need

9 in x 13 in (18 cm x 28 cm)
baking pan • Large saucepan
Wooden spoon • Spoon • Knife
Bowl • Saucepan • Wire rack

For plain oat bars

Butter for greasing baking pan

 1 cup (225 g) butter

½ cup (85 g) superfine sugar

2 tablespoons maple syrup or honey

3 cups (340 g) oatmeal

¼ teaspoon salt

For chocolate oat bars

4 oz (115 g) semisweet chocolate

For fruit-and-nut oat bars

1 cup (115 g) raisins

½ cup (55 g) sliced almonds

Plain oat bars

1 Preheat the oven. *Grease* the baking pan. Put the butter, sugar, and maple syrup or honey in a pan and melt over low heat.

2 Take the pan off the heat. Add the oats and salt to the butter mixture and mix everything together well.

3 Tip the mixture into the baking pan and press it down firmly. *Bake* for 20 to 30 minutes until golden brown.

4 Let the bars cool slightly, then cut them into squares. Once they have completely cooled take them out of the pan.

Chocolate oat bars

1 Make plain oat bars as above. Then break the chocolate into a bowl and stand it over a saucepan of water.

2 Heat the saucepan of water until it *simmers*. Stir the chocolate as it melts until it forms a smooth chocolate sauce.

3 Dip one end of each piece of oat bar into the melted chocolate, then put it on a wire rack until the chocolate sets.

78

Fruit-and-nut oat bars

Raisins, almonds, and oats make fruit-and-nut oat bars an energy-packed snack.

Make as for the plain oat bars, but add the raisins and almonds to the mixture at the same time as the oats and salt.

An oaty treat

Oat bars make a good snacktime treat. Make them late in the morning, and they will be ready to eat in the afternoon.

Chocolate oat bar

Plain oat bar

Fruit-and-nut oat bar

STAINED-GLASS COOKIES

You will need

Cookie sheet • Waxed paper
Mixing bowl • Wooden spoon
Sieve • Rolling pin • Cookie cutters
Sharp knife • Wire rack

Ingredients

½ cup (120 g) softened butter

¼ cup (55 g) superfine sugar

1½ cup (175 g) all-purpose flour

1-2 tablespoons milk

Fruit-flavored hard candies, broken-up

What to do

1 Preheat the oven. Line a cookie sheet with waxed paper. *Beat* the butter and sugar until thick, pale, and creamy.

2 *Sift* in the flour, then mix it into the butter and sugar. Stir in the milk, then knead to form a soft ball of dough.

3 *Roll out* the dough on a floured surface until about ¼ in (½ cm) thick, then cut it into shapes with cookie cutters.

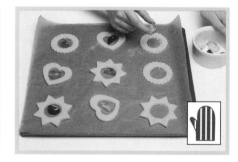

4 Cut a small hole in the middle of each shape and put broken-up candy in it. Bake the cookies for about 15 minutes until golden.

The cookie holds the candy in shape.

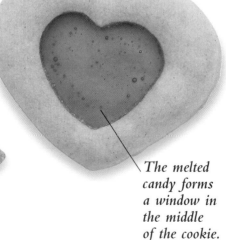

The melted candy forms a window in the middle of the cookie.

5 Take the cookies out of the oven. When the melted candies harden, move the cookies to a wire rack to finish cooling.

CHOCOLATE DIPS

You will need

*Cookie sheet • Waxed paper
Mixing bowl • Wooden spoon
Piping bag with medium-sized
star nozzle • Wire rack
Small bowl • Saucepan*

Ingredients

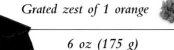 1 cup (225 g) softened butter

½ cup (55 g)
confectioners' sugar

1½ (175 g) all-purpose flour

¼ cup (55 g) cornstarch

Few drops vanilla extract

Grated zest of 1 orange

6 oz (175 g)
semisweet chocolate

Handy hints

If you haven't got a piping bag,
place widely spaced teaspoons
of the cookie mixture on the
cookie sheet instead.

What to do

1 Preheat the oven and line a cookie sheet with waxed paper. *Cream* the butter and sugar together in a mixing bowl.

2 Add the flour, cornstarch, vanilla extract, and orange zest to the butter mixture and *beat* well with a wooden spoon.

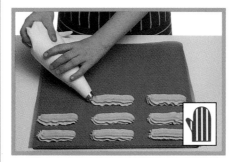

3 Put the mixture in a piping bag and pipe it onto the cookie sheet in short lines. *Bake* for 15 minutes until pale golden.

4 Cool the cookies on a wire rack. Break the chocolate into a small bowl and melt it over a pan of *simmering* water.

5 Dip one end of each cookie into the melted chocolate and lay it on the wire rack until the chocolate has set.

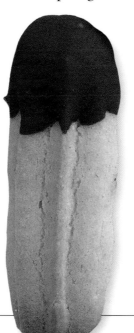

RASPBERRY MUFFINS

You will need

Paper cupcake liners • Muffin tin
Saucepan • Sieve • Bowl
Mixing bowl • Whisk or fork
Wooden spoon • Large metal spoon
Spoon • Wire rack

Ingredients

 ½ cup (120 g) butter

 2 cups (285 g) all-purpose flour

1 tablespoon baking powder

Pinch of salt

 2 eggs

½ cup (85 g) sugar

1 cup (220 ml) milk

 1 cup (225 g) raspberries

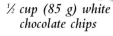 ½ cup (85 g) white chocolate chips

Tasty tips

You can make all kinds of muffins.

• Try using 1 cup (225 g) blackberries, blueberries, or chopped apricots instead of the raspberries.

• Instead of white chocolate, try dark chocolate or chopped nuts.

• To make apple muffins, just add 2 peeled, chopped apples and 1 teaspoon ground cinnamon to the basic recipe.

What to do

1 Preheat oven. Put cupcake liners in a muffin tin. Melt the butter. *Sift* the flour, salt, and baking powder into a bowl.

2 *Beat* the eggs in a bowl, then add the sugar, milk, and melted butter. Add the flour mixture and *fold* it in.

3 *Fold* the raspberries and chocolate chips into the muffin mixture, then spoon it into the cupcake liners.

4 *Bake* the muffins for 25 to 30 minutes until they rise and are firm and brown. Put them on a wire rack to cool.

The finished muffins are light and puffy.

Muffins are best eaten the day you make them.

PECAN PUFFS

You will need

2 cookie sheets • Mixing bowl
Wooden spoon • Coffee grinder, food
processor, or cutting board and
sharp knife • Sieve • Small sieve
or tea strainer • Wire rack

Ingredients

Butter for greasing cookie sheets

 ½ cup (115 g) softened
butter

2 tablespoons superfine sugar

 1¼ cup (140 g) pecan
or walnuts

1¼ cup (140 g)
all-purpose flour

A few drops vanilla extract

Confectioners' sugar
for dusting

What to do

1 Preheat the oven and *grease* the cookie sheets. *Beat* the butter in a bowl until soft, then *beat* in the sugar until creamy.

2 Chop the nuts very finely or grind them in a coffee grinder or food processor until they are like fine bread crumbs.

3 Stir the nuts into the butter and sugar, *sift* in the flour, then add the vanilla extract. Mix everything into a soft dough.

4 Roll the dough into balls about the size of walnuts and put them on the cookie sheets. *Bake* them for about 25 minutes.

Sift more confectioners' sugar over the pecan puffs once they have cooled.

5 *Sift* confectioners' sugar over the puffs and put them back in the oven for 2 minutes. Then put them on a wire rack to cool.

TEMPTING TARTS

You will need

*Sieve • Mixing bowl • Knife • Spoon
Plastic wrap • Rolling pin • Cookie
cutters • Muffin tin or tart pans • Wire
rack • Waxed paper • Baking pan
Pie weights • Cutting board
Sharp knife • Bowl • Whisk*

For the pastry

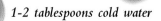

2 cups (225 g)
all-purpose flour

Pinch of salt

½ cup (120 g) butter

1 tablespoon sugar

1 beaten egg yolk

1-2 tablespoons cold water

For the jam tarts

Strawberry jam

Apricot jam

For the fruit tarts

A variety of soft fruit

⅔ cup (150 ml)
heavy cream

1½ teaspoons
confectioners' sugar

Handy hints

• To make it easier to line
the tart pans, scrunch up the
waxed paper first, then
open it out again.

• To make the tarts really
quickly, use ready-made
pie dough.

Making the pastry

1 *Sift* the flour and salt into the mixing bowl. Cut the butter into small pieces, then *cut* it into the flour with your fingertips.

2 When the mixture looks like bread crumbs, add the sugar and *beaten* egg. Mix in enough water to make a soft ball of dough.

3 Wrap the ball of dough in plastic wrap and put it in the refrigerator for 30 minutes. This will make it easier to *roll out*.

4 Set the oven. *Roll out* the pastry on a floured surface, then use a cookie cutter to cut out round shapes for the tarts.

Making the jam tarts

1 Lay the rounds of pastry in a muffin tin and press them gently into place. Spoon apricot or strawberry jam into them.

2 Decorate the tarts with pastry shapes. Bake for about 15 minutes until the pastry is golden brown, then cool on a wire rack.

Making the fruit tarts

1 Make pastry and line the tart pans with it. Line the pastry cases with waxed paper and pie weights. *Bake* for 15 minutes.

2 Let the pastry cases cool. Wash and slice the fruit, then whip the cream and confectioners' sugar together in a bowl until stiff.

3 Fill each pastry case with whipped cream, then arrange two or three types of sliced fruit in patterns on top.

Heavenly tarts

These tarts make a delicious afternoon treat, or you could serve the fruit tarts as a dessert.

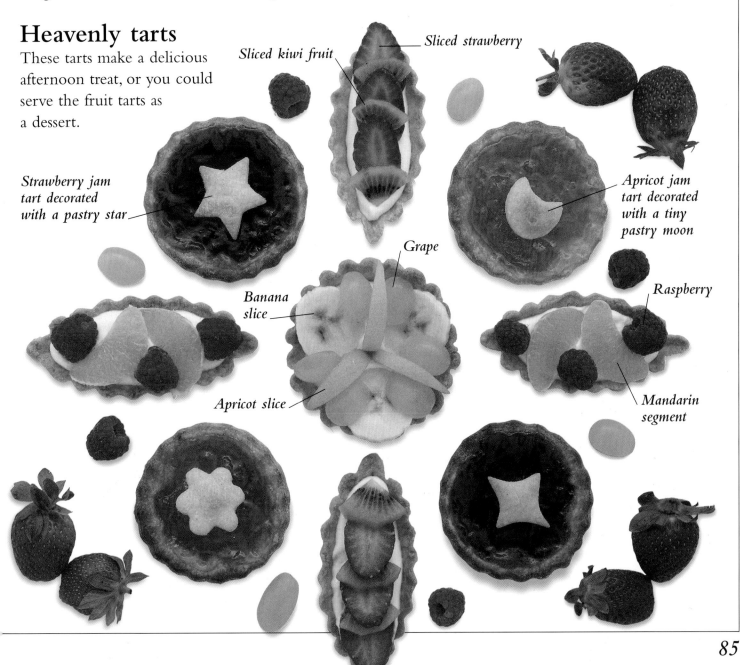

Sliced kiwi fruit

Sliced strawberry

Strawberry jam tart decorated with a pastry star

Apricot jam tart decorated with a tiny pastry moon

Grape

Banana slice

Raspberry

Apricot slice

Mandarin segment

85

FLORENTINES

You will need

Cookie sheet • Waxed paper
Cutting board • Sharp knife
Saucepan • Wooden spoon
Teaspoon • Wire rack • Bowl • Fork

Ingredients

 ½ *cup (55 g) sliced almonds*

¼ *cup (55 g) candied cherries*

4 tablespoons butter

¼ *cup (55 g) superfine sugar*

 ¼ *cup (55 g) candied peel*

1 tablespoon heavy cream

 4 oz (115 g) semisweet chocolate

What to do

1 Set the oven and line a cookie sheet. Chop the nuts and cherries finely. Melt the butter in a saucepan, then add the sugar.

2 When the sugar dissolves, *boil* the mixture for 1 minute. Take the pan off the heat. Mix in the nuts, cherries, peel, and cream.

3 Put teaspoons of the mixture onto the cookie sheet, then *bake* for 10 to 12 minutes until golden brown. Let cool.

4 Melt the chocolate in a bowl over a saucepan of *simmering* water. Spread the chocolate onto the backs of the florentines.

Use a fork to draw wavy lines in the melted chocolate.

CHOCOLATE CRISPY CAKES

You will need

*Large bowl • Large saucepan
Wooden spoon • Teaspoon
12 cupcake liners • Cookie sheet*

Ingredients

8 oz (225 g)
milk chocolate

*About 4 cups
(75 g) cornflakes
or puffed rice*

What to do

1 Melt the chocolate in a bowl over a saucepan of *simmering* water. Stir the chocolate from time to time until it is smooth.

2 Add the breakfast cereal to the melted chocolate and stir until the cereal and chocolate are mixed evenly.

The chocolate crispy cakes take about 1 hour to set.

3 Spoon the mixture into the cupcake liners. Put them on a cookie sheet and let stand in a cool place until the chocolate sets.

Store the crispy cakes in an airtight container to keep them fresh.

CHOCOLATE TRUFFLES

You will need

Mixing bowl • Wooden spoon
3 plates or shallow bowls
Paper candy liners

For the truffles

¼ cup (55 g)
cream or curd cheese

½ cup (55 g)
chopped nuts

½ cup (55 g)
confectioners' sugar

¼ cup (30 g)
cocoa powder

For the coating

Cocoa powder

Dried coconut

Chocolate sprinkles

What to do

1 Put the cream cheese, chopped nuts, confectioners' sugar, and cocoa powder in a bowl and mix together.

2 Put the cocoa, coconut, and sprinkles for the coating on three plates or shallow bowls. Roll the mixture into small balls.

3 Roll the truffles in the cocoa powder, coconut, or sprinkles, to coat them. Put the truffles in paper candy liners.

Chocolate truffle coated in cocoa powder

Chocolate truffle coated in dried coconut

Chocolate truffle coated in chocolate sprinkles

FRUIT-AND-NUT BALLS

You will need

Cookie sheet • Waxed paper • Cutting board and sharp knife, or food processor Bowl • Saucepan • Wooden spoon Paper candy liners

Ingredients

⅓ cup (85 g) dried apricots

½ cup (55 g) blanched almonds

⅓ cup (55 g) raisins

5 oz (140 g) white chocolate

⅓ cup (55 g) dried coconut

What to do

1 Line a cookie sheet with waxed paper. Chop the raisins, apricots, and almonds very finely, or whizz them in a food processor.

2 Melt the chocolate in a bowl over a saucepan of *simmering* water. Then stir in the chopped fruit, almonds, and coconut.

3 Roll the mixture into small balls. Put the balls on the cookie sheet and let them set for 1 to 2 hours.

The balls make a good after-dinner treat.

When the treats have set, put them in paper cupcake liners.

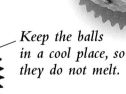
Keep the balls in a cool place, so they do not melt.

PEANUT BUTTER TREATS

You will need

Saucepan • Mixing bowl or food processor • Wooden spoon 8 in (20 cm) square baking pan Butter knife • Bowl • Sharp knife

For the treats

 4 tablespoons butter

 ⅓ cup (55 g) dark brown sugar

 8½ oz (240 g) smooth peanut butter

Scant 2 cups (200 g) confectioners' sugar

For the chocolate topping

1 cup (175 g) dark chocolate or chocolate chips

1 tablespoon butter

What to do

1 Melt the butter in a saucepan. Mix it in a bowl with the brown sugar, peanut butter, and confectioners' sugar.

2 Spoon the mixture into the baking pan and spread it out evenly. Press it down firmly on top with a butter knife.

3 Break the chocolate into a bowl and add the butter. Stir over a saucepan of *simmering* water until they melt.

4 Spread the chocolate over the peanut butter mixture. Let it chill until it has set but is still soft enough to cut.

Keep the peanut butter treats in the refrigerator until you are ready to eat them.

Peanut butter treats are good served at a birthday party.

5 Cut the mixture into squares and remove them from the baking pan, then put them in the refrigerator to finish setting.

PEPPERMINT CREAMS

You will need

Cookie sheet • Waxed paper
Mixing bowl • Whisk
Sieve • Wooden spoon • Fork
Bowl • Saucepan

Ingredients

 1 egg white

 3 cups (340 g) confectioners' sugar

 A few drops peppermint extract

A few drops each red and green food coloring (optional)

2 oz (55 g) semisweet chocolate

Tasty tip

Try making orange or lemon creams. Use half a teaspoon of orange or lemon juice instead of the peppermint extract.

What to do

1 Line a cookie sheet with waxed paper. *Whisk* the egg white lightly in a bowl until it is frothy but not stiff.

2 *Sift* the confectioners' sugar into the bowl, then stir it into the egg white until the mixture is stiff.

3 Knead in the peppermint extract. Divide the mixture into three balls. Knead food coloring into two of them.

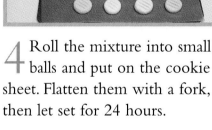

4 Roll the mixture into small balls and put on the cookie sheet. Flatten them with a fork, then let set for 24 hours.

5 Melt the chocolate in a bowl over a pan of *simmering* water. Dip some of the set peppermint creams into the chocolate.

Chocolate-dipped peppermint cream

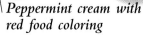

Lemon cream with yellow food coloring

Peppermint cream with green food coloring

Peppermint cream with red food coloring

Orange cream with orange food coloring

PICTURE GLOSSARY

This is a picture guide to some of the special terms that cooks often use. Here you can find out what each term means and learn to master the most useful basic cookery skills.

Grilling

To grill food, cook it quickly at a high temperature under a broiler. It is best to preheat the broiler before cooking the food.

Baking

Baking means cooking food in an oven. Turn on the oven in advance so that it is at the right temperature when you start baking.

Seasoning

To season food, add salt, pepper, spices, or herbs to it. This gives it extra flavor. Taste the food to check if it has enough seasoning.

Frying

Frying means cooking food in a shallow layer of hot fat or oil until it is crisp and golden. Food is usually fried in a frying pan.

Simmering

Simmering means cooking the ingredients over low heat on top of the stove so that the liquid is just bubbling.

Marinating

Marinating means soaking food in a sauce called a marinade before cooking. A marinade adds flavor and makes the food more tender.

Stir-frying

To stir-fry food, cook it in a wok or large frying pan with a little oil. Cook it over high heat and stir it all the time.

Boiling

Boiling means cooking the ingredients over high heat on top of the stove so that the liquid bubbles fiercely.

Dicing

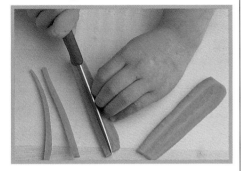

1 Dicing means cutting food into small cubes. To dice a vegetable, cut it in half lengthwise, then cut it into narrow strips.

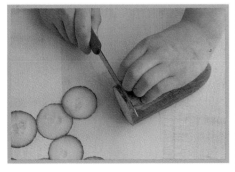

2 Hold the strips together firmly and slice across them, making small cubes. Move your fingers back carefully as you cut.

Slicing

To slice vegetables, hold them firmly on a cutting board and slice downward. Hold the knife against your knuckles, as shown.

Chopping an onion

1 Peel the papery skin off the onion. Leaving the root on will help hold the onion together when you slice it.

2 Cut the onion in half through the root. Lay one half cut side down and slice downward using a sharp knife.

3 When you have cut the onion in slices one way, turn the onion and cut across the first slices at right angles.

Shredding lettuce

Hold the lettuce down on a cutting board and cut across it in fine slices. This will give you thin ribbons of lettuce.

Chopping herbs

To chop fresh herbs, bunch the stalks together and hold them down on a cutting board, then slice across the leaves very finely.

Preparing ginger

Cut the woody skin off the piece of ginger. Slice the ginger finely. Cut the slices into thin strips, then cut the strips into small cubes.

Pitting fruit

1 Cut the fruit in half, following the crease down its side. Then twist each half of the fruit to loosen it from the pit.

2 The halves of the fruit will come apart, leaving one half with the pit. Scoop out the pit using a small spoon.

Separating an egg

1 Crack the egg near the middle by tapping it sharply against a bowl. Then break the egg open with your thumbs.

Coring an apple

1 Wash the apple, then hold it on a cutting board. Push the corer into it over the stalk, then push it down to the base.

2 Gently pull the corer out of the apple again. It will contain a cylinder of apple, including the core and the seeds.

2 Pour the yolk from one half of the shell to the other, so that the white slips into the bowl below. Put the yolk in a separate bowl.

Beating

To beat something means to stir it hard. Beat eggs with a fork or whisk until the yolks and whites are mixed together completely.

Whisking

To whisk egg whites, beat them lightly and quickly with a whisk or electric mixer until they are firm and stand up in little peaks.

Folding in

This is a gentle way of mixing two things together. Take scoops of the mixture and turn it over and around until it is mixed evenly.

Sifting

To sift flour or confectioners' sugar, shake it through a sieve. This gets rid of any lumps and makes the flour or sugar light and airy.

Cutting in

Cut the butter into cubes, then rub it into the flour with your fingertips until the mixture looks like bread crumbs.

Greasing a pan

To grease a cake pan or an ovenproof dish, rub it lightly with butter, oil, or lard. This stops food from sticking to it.

Creaming

1 To cream butter and sugar together, cut up softened butter and mix it with the sugar in a bowl using a wooden spoon.

2 Then beat the butter and sugar together hard until the mixture is pale and creamy and drops off the spoon easily.

Rolling out pastry

1 Sprinkle the table and rolling pin lightly with flour. Flatten the ball of pastry with your hand, then roll it out away from you.

2 Turn the pastry and roll it again, sprinkling it with flour if it sticks. Do this until the pastry is the shape and thickness needed.

Lining a cake pan

1 Lay the cake pan on a piece of waxed paper and draw around it. Then cut out the paper shape inside the line.

2 Brush the inside of the pan or sheet with melted butter, lay the waxed paper inside, and brush with more melted butter.

INDEX